I0571441

DIVORCING A NARCISSIST

A SEVEN-STEP BLUEPRINT TO UNDERSTAND YOUR TOXIC RELATIONSHIP, HEAL FROM EMOTIONAL ABUSE, AND SET HEALTHY BOUNDARIES TO REBUILD YOUR LIFE WITH CONFIDENCE

NORA W. HUNTER

© **Copyright 2024 - All rights reserved.**

The content contained within this book may not be reproduced, duplicated or transmitted without direct written permission from the author or the publisher.

Under no circumstances will any blame or legal responsibility be held against the publisher, or author, for any damages, reparation, or monetary loss due to the information contained within this book, either directly or indirectly.

Legal Notice:

This book is copyright protected. It is only for personal use. You cannot amend, distribute, sell, use, quote or paraphrase any part, or the content within this book, without the consent of the author or publisher.

Disclaimer Notice:

Please note the information contained within this document is for educational and entertainment purposes only. All effort has been executed to present accurate, up to date, reliable, complete information. No warranties of any kind are declared or implied. Readers acknowledge that the author is not engaged in the rendering of legal, financial, medical or professional advice. The content within this book has been derived from various sources. Please consult a licensed professional before attempting any techniques outlined in this book.

By reading this document, the reader agrees that under no circumstances is the author responsible for any losses, direct or indirect, that are incurred as a result of the use of the information contained within this document, including, but not limited to, errors, omissions, or inaccuracies.

CONTENTS

Introduction   5

1. SEEING THEM FOR WHO THEY TRULY ARE   11
   Step 1–(F) Face Reality   12
   More About the Different Kinds of Narcissists   19
   Facing the Hard Truth   23
   Breakout Box: Acceptance is the First Step to
   Healing   25

2. PICKING UP THE PIECES   29
   Step 2—(R) Rejuvenate Your Spirit   30
   Breakout Box: Unlocking Your Healing Journey   43

3. YOU'RE MORE THAN WHAT THEY MADE
   YOU FEEL   47
   Step 3—(E)levate Your Self-Worth   48
   Breakout Box: Rediscovering Your Worth   58

4. IT'S OKAY TO SAY NO   61
   Step 4—(E)mpower Through Boundaries   62
   Interactive Breakout Box: Navigating Boundaries
   With Narcissists   71

5. PREPARING FOR BATTLE, BUT HOPING FOR
   PEACE   75
   Step 5—(D)etermine Your Legal Strategy   76
   Interactive Element: Breakout Box   92

6. KEEPING THE KIDS' BEST INTERESTS AT
   HEART   95
   Step 6—(O)utline Parallel Parenting Plans   96
   Breakout Box: Your Child's Wellbeing Comes First   111

7. A FUTURE WHERE YOU'RE TRULY FREE   113
Step 7—(M)ove Forward   115
Breakout Box: Opening Up to the Future   128
Life After Freedom: Rebuilding Goals Worksheet   129

Conclusion   135
Epilogue: A Love Letter   139
Appendix: Communication Toolkit   143
References   151

Introduction

I want to start this journey with you by first acknowledging the heavy weight that you carry in your heart. It's not lost on me—the pain, confusion, and isolation you may be feeling as you navigate the tough journey of divorcing a narcissist. If you're holding this book in your hands right now, understand that it's not a coincidence. You've taken a brave step, and I want you to recognize the courage it took to even open these pages.

I am writing to you as a friend because, in the pages that lie ahead, that's exactly what we're going to become: travel mates on the journey toward healing, mental and physical stamina, and rediscovery. In my own failed relationship, I've seen the weathering of trust, felt the emotional trauma and isolation, and faced legal battles similar to what you may be grappling with. And I want you to know you're not alone.

I grew up in a small town where some people took really good care of each other while others gossiped up a storm. I've always been interested in why people act the way they do. I also have a strong desire to support others when they face difficult situations in life. But I never expected that my own life would lead me into the complicated world of being married to a narcissistic person.

At first, it seemed like a great match. Still, I ended up in a terrible relationship that became emotionally abusive over time. The person who initially charmed me started manipulating and gaslighting me, which made me doubt myself and my sanity. It was really hard, but I finally found the courage to make the tough choice to get a divorce.

The time after my divorce was a period of significant change for me. I started learning about psychology, recovering from trauma, and understanding narcissistic personality disorder. I combined my personal experiences with what I could learn from formal resources to gain a deeper understanding. It wasn't an easy journey, but it made me stronger and wiser, and I felt a strong desire to share what I had learned.

I don't claim to have all the answers, but my intimate understanding of the challenges posed by narcissistic relationships, coupled with a commitment to ongoing learning, has driven me to offer support to others facing similar struggles.

In *Divorcing a Narcissist*, I aim to share insights from my own hard-earned lessons. The seven-step blueprint is not a boastful declaration but rather a humble offering based on my personal experience, knowledge, and deep sense of empathy. I want you to know that you are NOT ALONE. There is a path toward understanding, healing, and rebuilding your confidence after the turmoil of your relationship with a narcissist.

Through this book, I hope to extend a guiding hand to you if you are seeking to break free. I want to provide you with a source of support as you start on your very own journey of self-discovery and recovery.

Divorcing a Narcissist is more than just a guide through the practicalities of divorce. It's a safe space for you—a refuge where we'll navigate the flood of emotions together. I understand that divorcing a narcissist isn't just about breaking free from legal ties; it's about reclaiming your identity, rebuilding your emotional well-being, developing your self-confidence, and charting a course toward a future that's truly yours.

Maybe it was a quiet night when you felt overwhelmed by betrayal and broken trust. Or perhaps it was a day when you couldn't bear the loneliness and isolation anymore. You might have picked up this book during a moment of deep thinking, realizing that you needed more than just legal advice. Maybe you were looking for understanding, empathy, and guidance for emotional healing. It's possible that you heard a faint whisper in your own voice saying, *There must be more to this journey than just fighting in court.* Whatever brought you here, I want to congratulate you on taking the courageous first step toward reclaiming your life.

I get it. I see you.

You didn't choose this book because it promised a quick fix or an easy solution. You chose it because you're ready for a journey—a journey that acknowledges your emotional trauma, the struggles of co-parenting (if you have children with the narcissist), and your fear of an uncertain future.

In these pages, we'll tackle the tough stuff—the betrayals that cut deep, the emotional wounds that need healing, and the loneliness that seems insurmountable. But we'll also cheer for the wins, even the tiny ones, as you rediscover the strong and resilient person inside of you.

Now, let me introduce you to our toolkit, "The Path to F.R.E.E.D.O.M."—a roadmap that will guide you through the transformative journey that lies ahead:

- **F—Face reality:** We start by acknowledging the truth. Facing reality is the first step toward reclaiming control over your life.
- **R—Rejuvenate your spirit:** Rediscover the essence of who you are. Rejuvenate your spirit by reconnecting with your passions, values, and dreams.
- **E—Elevate your self-worth:** It's time to rebuild your self-esteem. Elevate your self-worth and recognize the strength within you that transcends the challenges you've faced.
- **E—Empower through boundaries:** Establishing boundaries is a powerful tool in dealing with narcissistic behavior. Learn how to set and enforce boundaries that protect your well-being.
- **D—Determine your legal strategy:** Knowledge is power, especially in legal matters. Determine your legal approach with confident and clear decisions.
- **O—Outline co-parenting plans:** Navigate co-parenting challenges with a well-defined plan. Ensure stability and support for your children while safeguarding your own peace of mind.
- **M—Move forward:** Moving forward is your ultimate goal. Embrace the future with courage, resilience, and the newfound freedom to live life on your terms.

Using the above roadmap, you'll gain insights and strategies to navigate your unique challenges, moving swiftly from pain to empowerment. Take note, even though the title refers to divorce, the information in this book will also be helpful if you were in a long-term relationship with a narcissist—maybe you were never married but have children together. You will still want to read this book, as it contains advice that may be helpful for you too.

This journey won't always be easy. I won't sugarcoat the challenges you'll face, but I can promise you this: it will be worth it. As we explore the intricacies of divorcing a narcissist, we'll also unearth the strength within you that perhaps you didn't know existed. We'll find the tools for not just surviving but thriving in the aftermath.

So, my friend, buckle up for a journey of self-discovery, empowerment, and healing. You're not just divorcing a narcissist; you're reclaiming your life. And together, we'll walk this path—one page at a time.

1. Seeing Them for Who They Truly Are

Emma's heart raced as she thought back to the whirlwind romance that had completely swept her off her feet. David, with his irresistible charm and the way he made her feel incredibly special, had won her heart right from the start. Their extravagant wedding reception had become the talk of the town—like a real-life fairy tale.

But as time passed, Emma began to notice small cracks in their seemingly perfect life. David's constant need for control, from deciding where they went to choosing her outfits, started to raise concerns. The extravagant gifts and surprise trips that used to feel like expressions of love now seemed like manipulative tactics.

Emma's friends, who had once admired their seemingly perfect relationship, started expressing worries. From Emma's changed behavior, they could see David seemed possessive and self-centered, and something was wrong. Emma couldn't ignore the mounting evidence any longer.

The breaking point came when David tried to isolate her from her family, claiming they were "jealous" of their love. At that moment, Emma's eyes were opened to the truth. The dream life she had believed in was nothing more than a carefully constructed facade by a narcissistic person.

With a heavy heart, Emma realized she needed to gather the strength to break free from David's controlling grip. It was time to see him for who he truly was and reclaim her own identity. Little did she know, this journey would test her resilience, challenge her beliefs, and ultimately lead her to a newfound sense of empowerment.

This marked the beginning of Emma's brave first step to escape the web of narcissism that had ensnared her. The journey would forever change her life as she embarked on a path of self-discovery, healing, and liberation.

Emma's story is a testament to her incredible bravery in recognizing and admitting the signs of narcissism early in her marriage. Sadly, many women fail to do so or choose to ignore them out of fear or a lack of self-confidence. Emma's journey toward self-empowerment and healing serves as a reminder that being aware of these signs can spare us from a world of heartache and manipulation. It is a powerful testimony to the courage and determination of those who refuse to be overpowered by narcissistic behavior.

Now, join me on the path to F.R.E.E.D.O.M. Let's explore the very first step.

STEP 1–(F) FACE REALITY

Being married to a narcissist can be really tough and affect you in many ways. The first step is to face reality and acknowledge how your partner is impacting you. A narcissistic spouse is usually manipulative, self-centered, complex to connect with, and maybe verbally aggressive or abusive.

When you are in a close relationship with a narcissist, they will make you feel bad about yourself, make it harder for you to have lasting connections with others, limit your ability to obtain the necessary funds to exit the relationship, and trigger issues with your mental health due to the abuse.

It's essential to recognize your own needs and wants, nurture other healthy relationships, and ensure you're getting the support you need. It is not your job to fix your spouse; instead, express your demands and make an effort to look after yourself.

You need to have control over your finances, save some money secretly, or have a source of income that the narcissist doesn't know about—and be kind to yourself. Lastly, it's crucial to learn healthy ways to deal with and protect yourself from the narcissist. This includes recognizing manipulation, building healthy relationships, managing expectations, setting clear boundaries, choosing your battles wisely, staying true to yourself, and finding a good therapist. This chapter is all about recognizing what a narcissist is and how they operate, so you will be sure you start facing the reality if your spouse falls within these descriptions.

The Magnetic Pull of a Narcissist

With lavish gifts and early "I love you's," narcissists are sneaky humans who have an extraordinary talent for making people feel really special and unique when they first meet. They love being the center of attention, going all out to impress others and make them feel like they're the most important person in the world.

They shower their targets with compliments, talk about soulmates, and even say "I love you" way too soon. They're really good at copying the behavior of the person they're interested in and giving them lots of attention. They're also great storytellers. But here's the thing: all this charm is actually a sneaky plan to get admiration and control because narcissists are all about themselves.

So don't beat yourself up if you've fallen for a narcissist. They can be really charming and captivating, making you feel incredibly special in the whirlwind of their attention. When you're with a narcissist, it's crucial to identify how your partner is influencing you, to realize your own needs and goals, to cultivate other healthy connections, and to make sure you're receiving the support you require (Holland, 2022).

In order to have any chance of fixing a troubled relationship with a narcissistic person, the narcissists themselves must work on changing their self-centered and negative behaviors. They should try to break free from their self-absorbed habits and the belief that they don't need anyone else. They need to learn how to understand and respect other people's feelings. Lastly, they should strive to have goals that go beyond their own interests and genuinely care about the wellness of others. Acts of generosity and kindness toward others can help them build genuine self-esteem and learn to focus on others instead of just themselves. If a narcissist promises to change their behavior, it should show in the way they act, or it means it was all another trick to keep you stuck in their web.

Secret Agendas

Narcissists have secret plans behind their initial charm. They often use their attractive behavior to manipulate and control others, driven by a constant need for admiration, validation, and power. Their acts of generosity and helpfulness may be a mask to increase their social influence, make new connections, and gain access to more resources. Moreover, narcissists may help others with the intention of keeping them indebted for the future, thus maintaining power over them. Their attraction is superficial and serves their own agenda rather than genuinely caring for others. It's important to understand that the initial attraction of a narcissist is not based on genuine empathy or care but rather on their self-centered motives and the desire for control and admiration.

Common Behaviors

Because narcissists are challenging to diagnose and even more tricky to treat, there are many of them walking the streets without us even knowing. You should know about some general behaviors of narcissists in relationships (Firestone, 2013; Grande, 2022; Biggers, 2022; Kassel, 2022; Villines, 2023).

Key traits and behaviors that define narcissism include these examples:

- **They feel you owe them all your time:** Narcissists often believe they should be treated differently and think they are superior to others.
- **They lack compassion in the relationship:** It's hard for them to understand and care about other people's feelings. They focus on their own needs and can seem cold and distant when their partner needs emotional support.
- **They manipulate and control you:** Narcissists may use tactics like making their partner doubt their own sanity, making them feel guilty, or trying to control them.
- **They exaggerate their achievements:** They may brag about their accomplishments and take credit for things they didn't really do or even for things that their spouse did!

- **They ignore your feelings:** Narcissists often don't pay attention to their partner's emotions and needs. They mainly focus on what they want.
- **They use the relationship to only benefit themselves:** They might take advantage of their partner or use the relationship to get what they want.
- **They idealize you at first, but later they treat you like *#%@:** In the beginning, narcissists can make their partner feel really special and loved. This is called the idealization stage. This dynamic changes later on.
- **Feeling of self-importance:** Narcissists think they're really important and believe they're one-of-a-kind or special.
- **Being consumed by visual appeal, influence, control, or success:** They really like it when people admire and pay attention to them. They always look for chances to show off or talk about their accomplishments.
- **Manipulative or controlling behavior:** Narcissists try to maintain control over their partners and may exploit them for their own gain.
- **Strong need for admiration:** They constantly seek validation and recognition from others.
- **Focus on their own needs:** Narcissists often prioritize their own needs over those of their partners, leaving the other person feeling unheard and uncared for.
- **Higher levels of aggression:** They may lash out when their needs are not met or when they feel they have been slighted.
- **Difficulty accepting feedback:** Narcissists often struggle to accept criticism and may make their partners question their memories or sanity.

- **Superficial charm:** They may be captivating and charming, especially at the beginning of a relationship.
- **Cold and detached behavior:** Narcissists may seem disinterested or unavailable when their partners need emotional support.
- **Extreme sensitivity to criticism:** They may become defensive or aggressive when faced with constructive feedback.
- **Exploitation:** Narcissists may manipulate their partners into doing things for their benefit, such as lying about them to others or harming their reputation.

It's important to know that these behaviors can vary in how strong they are and how much they affect the relationship. If you're in a relationship with someone who shows narcissistic behavior, it's a good idea to seek help from a professional.

The Rollercoaster of Emotions

The emotional journey in a relationship with a narcissist is often characterized by a tumultuous cycle, as outlined by various sources. The idealization phase, also known as the love bombing stage, is marked by an otherworldly emotional high, where the narcissist elevates their partner to soaring heights, making them feel like they have found their soulmate and can't believe their good fortune. This phase is characterized by excessive compliments, attention, and affection, creating an intoxicating whirlwind of emotions.

However, this phase is often followed by the devaluation phase, where doubts and insecurities creep in, and the narcissist's facade crumbles, revealing a cruel and calculating nature. During this phase, the victim's self-esteem is systematically eroded, and they are subjected to emotional turmoil, criticism, and psychological wounds.

Finally, the victim is left feeling bewildered and wounded by the narcissist's sudden and cold-blooded withdrawal of their emotional support and cruel breakup.

This process can occur multiple times, resulting in an overwhelming cycle of emotional disorientation. The cycle of narcissistic abuse frequently includes ongoing idealization and devaluation, culminating in the abandonment of the victim, who is no longer the fresh, exciting object that initially made the narcissist feel special (Wakefield, 2023).

The emotional rollercoaster of a relationship with a narcissist can be chaotic, aggressive, and emotionally abusive, leaving the victim feeling alone, unheard, and uncared for. It is important to recognize and understand these patterns to break free from such a toxic cycle and seek support for recovery and healing.

When the Charm Stops

Narcissism is a fancy term for a personality trait that can appear in different forms (Raypole, 2021). It can range from having a good sense of self-worth to having narcissistic tendencies. To really understand what narcissism is and how it's different from healthy self-esteem, we need to look at the main traits and behaviors that define narcissism and how they affect our relationships with others. In relationships, narcissists often display behaviors that can harm their partners and the overall health of the relationship. These behaviors can make it challenging for partners to maintain a healthy and balanced relationship, often leading to feelings of isolation, confusion, and frustration.

There are different kinds of narcissism, and experts usually work with five main categories: covert, communal, antagonistic, overt, and malignant narcissism (Telloian, 2021). However, there are more types emerging like spiritual, sexual, parasitic, boomerang, and many others. In this book, we will focus on the five main categories.

Overt narcissism is when someone has a big ego and thinks highly of themselves. Covert narcissism is when someone is sensitive and easily hurt but still has a big ego. Antagonistic narcissism is when someone is mean and aggressive toward others, while communal narcissism is when someone wants to be praised for being selfless and helpful. Malignant narcissism is the most extreme form, where someone is arrogant, aggressive, and behaves in antisocial ways.

While there are different types of narcissism, narcissistic personality disorder (NPD) is a diagnosed mental health condition with more severe and pervasive symptoms (Caligor & Petrini, 2022) It needs to be treated seriously.

MORE ABOUT THE DIFFERENT KINDS OF NARCISSISTS

Narcissism is divided into two key categories (Telloian, 2021):

- **Adaptive (helpful):** When narcissistic traits are harnessed effectively, they can bring about positive qualities such as strong self-confidence, independence, and the ability to appreciate and celebrate one's accomplishments.
- **Maladaptive (not helpful):** The personality elements that are harmful to themselves and others include aggressiveness, misusing others, and a sense of entitlement. Yup, the world owes them something and everything, you know!

In the maladaptive category, five types of narcissists have been identified:

- antagonistic (agentic or grandiose)
- communal
- overt
- covert
- malignant

Narcissism can be a personality element or a formal mental diagnosis called narcissistic personality disorder (NPD). People may also have some narcissistic characteristics without having a complete personality disorder.

Let's find out more about each of these maladaptive behavior disorder styles.

Antagonistic Narcissists

- **Characteristics:** This type of narcissist is often characterized by grandiosity, an inflated sense of self-importance, and a constant need for admiration. Antagonistic narcissism is all about rivalry and competition. People with this type of narcissism often act arrogant and take advantage of others.
- **Behavior:** They may engage in arrogant and boastful behavior, exaggerate their achievements, showcase a sense of entitlement, and have a tendency to belittle or demean others to maintain their perceived superiority. They can quickly light up a room with their sociable and overbearing charm.

- **Interpersonal relationships:** Antagonistic narcissists often struggle with forming deep and meaningful connections, as their focus on their own needs and superiority can hinder genuine emotional intimacy. They sure know how to talk up a storm, but when it comes to listening, well, let's just say it's not their strong suit!

Communal Narcissists

- **Characteristics:** Unlike antagonistic narcissists, communal narcissists seek validation by appearing selfless and altruistic. They may present themselves as caring, generous, and empathetic.
- **Behavior:** Their acts of kindness and generosity may be motivated by a desire for admiration and recognition rather than genuine concern for others.
- **Interpersonal relationships:** While appearing caring, communal narcissists may still struggle with forming authentic connections as their altruistic actions are often driven by a need for external validation. Yup, they're putting on a good show!

Covert Narcissists

- **Characteristics:** Covert narcissists tend to be introverted and may not display the overt grandiosity seen in other types. Rather, they expect excessive admiration and have a persistent attitude of entitlement.
- **Behavior:** Their narcissism is often expressed through subtle forms of manipulation, passive-aggressive behavior, and a victim mentality.

- **Interpersonal relationships:** It's hard to identify covert narcissists because they disguise their narcissistic traits behind a mask of humility. They may have trouble building meaningful connections with others because they tend to manipulate people.

Malignant Narcissists

- **Characteristics:** Malignant narcissists exhibit a combination of narcissistic traits and antisocial behavior. They may be prone to aggression, sadism, and a lack of empathy.
- **Behavior:** Malignant narcissists can be particularly destructive, engaging in harmful actions toward others without remorse or empathy. They may exploit others for their own gain and disregard ethical or moral boundaries.
- **Interpersonal relationships:** Forming healthy relationships with a malignant narcissist is challenging due to their manipulative and often abusive behavior. They may exploit others for personal gain without regard for the well-being of those around them.

Each type of narcissist in the maladaptive category has its own unique way of showing narcissistic traits. These traits affect how they behave, interact with others, and impact those around them. It's important to remember that these categories are not fixed, and individuals can display a mix of traits from different types. Imagine it like a rainbow of narcissism, where a person can have a combination of different colors.

FACING THE HARD TRUTH

You've just realized that your spouse checks all the boxes on the complete narcissist checklist. Now what?

You might feel like you have lost a part of yourself, you might be struggling to figure out who you are, and you might even struggle with loving yourself without loving your spouse. If you are emotionally overwhelmed or a total wreck, welcome to the club of many of us —at least until we decide to lift our heads high and pick our lives back up from the floor.

Starting on this journey of realizing and accepting that your husband is a narcissist can be a challenging but transformative experience. It's like riding an emotional rollercoaster with ups and downs. But you may feel more down than up until you start healing and get to a place of joy and peace. Remember, making a vow to have no contact with your narcissist future ex-husband (if at all possible) is like grieving someone who has just died. You will experience many stages in the process before you accept the hard reality (Casabianca, 2021; Holland 2023):

- **Stage 1—Devastation:** At first, you may feel overwhelmed with emotions like shock and a deep sense of loss. It can be incredibly painful to realize that the person you love is not who you thought they were. Now, you are thinking, *I'm heartbroken, how could he do this to me? After all I have sacrificed for him?*
- **Stage 2—Denial:** During this phase, you might hope things will change or the narcissistic traits will disappear. Denial acts as a way to protect yourself from the harsh reality: *Maybe everything was a big misunderstanding, maybe my wife isn't that bad, maybe I should give her another chance.*

- **Stage 3—Anger:** As denial starts to fade away, anger takes its place. You may feel angry at the narcissist for their manipulative actions but also at yourself for not recognizing the signs earlier. This stage is essential for acknowledging your anger and finding healthy ways to channel it. You may think, *I can't believe I trusted him. I'm so foolish.*
- **Stage 4—Bargaining (Doubt):** Oh, please don't give in to this stage. You need to be strong. Doubt may creep in, making you question if leaving or distancing yourself is the right decision. Your mind might be overwhelmed with conflicting emotions and a need for reassurance. You might tell yourself, *Maybe if I approach things differently and give my spouse another chance, everything will be better.*
- **Stage 5—Depression:** A deep sense of sadness and mourning may settle in as you come to terms with the magnitude of the situation. It's critical to allow yourself to mourn the end of the relationship you had great dreams for. You may be thinking things such as, *I don't know how to move on with my life.*
- **Stage 6—Acceptance:** This is a turning point—accepting that the relationship was toxic and that it's time to move forward. The first step toward recovery and personal development is acceptance and admitting to yourself, *Leaving this relationship was the best thing I could do for my future self.*

The Shift Toward Growth

- **Stage 7—Forgiveness:** Forgiveness in this context doesn't mean absolving the narcissist of their actions. Instead, it means pardoning yourself. By forgiving yourself for being in the relationship, you allow healing to begin.

- **Stage 8—Awakening to hope:** This stage signifies a renewed sense of optimism. It's a belief that a brighter future awaits, free from the toxicity of the narcissistic relationship.
- **Stage 9—Self-discovery:** In this stage, you rediscover yourself, your passions, and your strengths. It's an opportunity for personal growth, building resilience, and establishing a stronger sense of identity.
- **Stage 10—Joy and peace:** This stage is the ultimate destination—achieving joy and peace. As you heal and grow, you regain control over your life and emotions. You may be scared for life, but it's a testimony of your true strength and resilience.

Your journey from complete devastation to joy and peace shows the incredible resilience of your human spirit. Recovering from a narcissistic relationship is a difficult undertaking. It requires self-compassion, time, patience, and persistence. But I know you have already been through a lot and will survive this, too. Take it one day at a time. It is possible to emerge from the shadows of a narcissistic relationship and find happiness and peace in your future.

BREAKOUT BOX: ACCEPTANCE IS THE FIRST STEP TO HEALING

This chapter was all about facing the reality of your narcissistic relationship and accepting that it's over and you need to move on with your life.

Acceptance is a crucial milestone in your journey of healing. It is that pivotal moment when you acknowledge and come to terms with the fact that the relationship you were in was toxic. Only by accepting this reality can you begin the process of healing and moving forward.

Acceptance doesn't mean forgetting or forgiving the pain caused by the relationship. It means facing the truth and freeing yourself from the emotional weight. It's not an easy thing to do, but it's the first step toward healing.

When you fully understand and embrace the truth of the situation, you regain your personal power and take control of your own life. This acceptance allows you to leave the past behind and be open to a future filled with possibilities. It's a declaration that you deserve better and are prepared to embark on a journey of healing and self-discovery.

Keep in mind that accepting things doesn't mean you're weak. It actually shows that you're strong and resilient. It's the first step toward healing, personal growth, and rediscovering happiness and peace in your life. Embrace acceptance, and you'll open doors to a better future.

Affirmations for Accepting That Your Relationship Is Over

Here are five affirmations to help you accept that the relationship is over:

- I understand that the relationship has ended, and I am excited about the chance to start fresh and grow as an individual.
- I am letting go of any attachment to the past and embracing the present moment with an open heart and mind.
- I deserve a healthy, loving, and supportive relationship, and I am prepared to create that for myself.
- I am choosing to release what no longer serves me and have faith that something wonderful is in store for my future.

- I am choosing to release what no longer benefits me and have faith that the universe has something wonderful in store for my future.

Say these positive statements daily to strengthen your belief and be open to the many opportunities waiting for you. Accepting yourself is the initial stage toward healing and building a better future.

———

Now that you have the tools for acceptance, we will move on to Chapter 2 to discuss how you can start your healing journey. Here's to "Picking up the Pieces."

2. Picking Up the Pieces

Becky met Ryan on a blind date. He was a dream catch. Ryan's confidence stood out like a breath of fresh air in a room full of people. His caring nature made Becky feel safe and secure. As their relationship progressed, his presence shielded her from life's ups and downs. But little did she realize that this shield would eventually become suffocating, making her feel trapped and unable to express herself within their marriage.

As time passed and their marriage fell apart, Becky found herself at a crossroads. It had been a while since she had been in a place where she could make decisions for herself. The choices she used to make confidently were now influenced by Ryan's criticisms. His hurtful words had damaged her self-esteem.

In her quest to find herself again, Becky rediscovered a childhood passion: drawing. The colorful strokes of her pencils on the canvas became a lifeline for her, helping her heal from the emotional wounds she carried. Each stroke allowed her to declare her independence and break free from the constraints that had held her back for so long.

In the peacefulness of her studio, Becky found her voice, one that had been silenced by the demands of her stifling relationship. Drawing women became more than just a hobby; it became a way for her to express her emotions and show her strength.

Despite the pain she had experienced, Becky found comfort, resilience, and a renewed sense of purpose. Through her art, she redefined herself, letting go of the weight of the past and embracing the freedom to be herself without apology. Her art became very popular because it also drew a story of hope for other women who knew what pain felt like.

This chapter of Becky's life unfolded not only on the canvas but in her journey as she drew her way back to the person she had once almost lost completely but finally found.

In this chapter, we will talk about healing after a narcissistic relationship. I hope the insights you find here will be of great help to you on your journey of healing, acceptance, and self-discovery.

STEP 2—(R) REJUVENATE YOUR SPIRIT

What is worse than divorcing from a narcissist? Yup, being married to one!

Just like in Becky's case, narcissistic abuse can take a toll on you, leaving you to feel bad about yourself. It can make you feel ashamed, have flashbacks to bad memories, and feel like you can't do anything right. The effects can last a long time and cause things like anxiety, sadness, and feeling stuck without a way out. It can also make it hard for you to know who you are and to make your own choices, and you may sometimes even do things to hurt yourself. You've been through a lot. You may feel exhausted and used up. The impact of narcissistic abuse can affect everything in your life, such as who you are, your health, and your current and future relationships. The emotional scars can be profound and stick around for a long time, affecting many parts of your life.

However, you must lift your head now because you are ready for what lies ahead. You are ready to embrace a new life, learn and grow, find happiness and peace within yourself, and finally rejuvenate your spirit.

The Deep Scars They Leave Behind

As a victim of narcissistic abuse, you may suffer from different traumatic reactions such as "freezing," "fleeing," "fighting," or "fawning."

You may either freeze in fear, leave to avoid the abuse, fight back, or fawn—try to make the narcissist happy. Being married to a narcissist can mess with your happiness and overall health, especially when you finally break free from them.

Let's take a look at the long-lasting emotional wounds that can happen after being in such a chaotic relationship (Holland, 2022; Gillis, 2023).

Difficulty to Move On With a Normal Life

If you are busy getting divorced but still living in the same house as your spouse, you need to leave. Please don't fool yourself by thinking it's okay to stay there. Remember, a narcissistic partner will look for any and every dirt they can get on you to use in the divorce proceedings, and they will most likely get an attorney who agrees with their approach. Don't engage. Get the divorce finalized as soon as possible, cut your losses, and move on. Below are some of the wounds inflicted that may prevent you from moving on with your life.

- **Low self-esteem:** Narcissists often undermine their partners' self-worth. After years of emotional manipulation and gaslighting, you may struggle with self-doubt and self-esteem issues.
- **Extinct healthy relationships:** Narcissists prioritize their personal needs and rarely empathize with others. Resulting from this, the number of close relationships in your life may have decreased since being involved with your spouse.
- **Being isolated from everyone and everything:** Narcissist abusers isolate their victims. The narcissist's need for control and your submissive response can cause your connections with friends, family, and support networks to deteriorate.
- **Limitations on accessing resources:** Narcissists may control your finances, isolate you from friends and family, and limit your available resources. After divorce, rebuilding your life can be challenging because of these restrictions.
- **Physical symptoms:** The toll on mental health can manifest physically in your body—insomnia, headaches, gastrointestinal issues, and stress-related ailments are some of the symptoms you may experience as a result of this.
- **Finding it hard to make choices:** Gaslighting and manipulation can leave you second-guessing yourself all the time. Even simple decisions become impossible to handle.
- **Self-destructive behaviors:** Some people cope by immersing themselves in self-destructive behaviors—like even more troubled relationships, self-injury, and substance misuse. You could find yourself doing this to dull your pain.
- **Sacrificing your needs:** Victims prioritize the narcissist's needs over their own. If this is true in your cause, you may feel emotionally depleted.

- **Struggling to trust and commit again:** Trust becomes fragile. Victims struggle to trust others, fearing betrayal or manipulation.

Long-Term Effects of Trauma on Your Emotions

As a survivor of narcissistic abuse, you may carry emotional trauma long after your relationship ends. This trauma can manifest as anxiety, hypervigilance, and a continuous sense of toxic shame. As you recognize the depth of emotional manipulation you have endured, you may experience shock and disbelief, realizing that someone you trusted with your life inflicted such great harm. Some of the long-term effects of trauma you may be experiencing are listed below (Cuncic, 2023; Gillis, 2023).

- **Feeling battered and drained:** Going on a long walk, imagine carrying a heavy backpack filled with emotional weight—the burden of constant criticism, gaslighting, and manipulation. Each step feels heavier, and the straps dig into your shoulders. The emotional exhaustion from being in a narcissistic relationship can leave you feeling battered and drained. The constant emotional turmoil could have taken its toll on you.
- **Emotionally "used up" and discarded:** Narcissists often discard their partners callously, leaving them feeling emotionally depleted and discarded. It's as if your emotional resources have been drained to the last drop.
- **Feeling traumatized and scared:** The fear of retaliation, ongoing legal battles, and the trauma from the relationship can haunt you even after divorce.
- **Shame and self-doubt:** You may internalize the narcissist's criticisms and blame yourself. Self-doubt and guilt become constant companions, eroding your self-esteem.

- **Guilt and insecurity:** You may start believing the narcissist's comments and criticize yourself. Self-doubt and regret may become your best friends daily, lowering your self-worth.
- **Breaking down your identity:** Narcissists undermine their partners' identity. It is possible to completely lose touch with your real personality and your life's greatest passions.
- **Failing to establish proper boundaries:** Even after the relationship ends, the line between what you want and deserve is blurry.
- **Challenges with mental well-being:** The emotional abuse you endured during your marriage can lead to anxiety, long-term sadness, and other mental health issues. Healing from these severe wounds takes time.
- **Uncertainty and being "on guard" 24/7:** The uninterrupted vigilance needed in a narcissistic relationship can make you feel always on your guard and anxious.
- **As a coping strategy victims disassociate:** To endure the mental storm, you may find yourself withdrawing from your feelings.
- **Self-gaslighting:** Internalizing the narcissist's distortions, you may start doubting your values and perceptions.
- **Trauma bonding:** Despite the abuse, you may feel bonded to the narcissist. The trauma bond keeps you tethered, even when logic dictates otherwise, and you may unfortunately consider going back into the relationship. This is a big no, no. Run!

Don't be hard on yourself. Healing from a narcissistic marriage is a process. Seek professional help, surround yourself with a supportive network, and prioritize self-care as you move forward. You deserve healing and freedom.

Prioritizing Your Emotional Health

A year ago, Eva, a 32-year-old mom of a five-year-old boy, was suddenly burdened with thousands of dollars of debt to pay off after requesting a divorce from Kyle. She didn't even know the term "narcissist" at that time. However, she did know one thing—placing herself in financial difficulty and devastating her son by getting a divorce and moving on their own would damage their lives much less than staying in the marriage would have.

For the sake of her and her son's emotional health, Eva decided co-parenting would be better than staying married. However, she had to learn how to teach her child to deal with the emotions of divorce and also how to cope with a narcissistic parent in their life on random weekends and holidays—because divorcing Kyle didn't change him.

Eva soon realized that she first had to learn how to prioritize and care for her emotional health before showing her son how to be emotionally healthy. However, learning to live independently from him helped Eva to grow and develop in her own right.

Nourishing Your Spirit

Let's talk about some healing techniques that can benefit you spiritually, help you with your emotional trauma, and promote your personal growth. Here are commonly used therapies and alternative methods for healing from narcissistic abuse (Laderer, n.d.; *Therapy for Narcissistic Abuse,* n.d.):

- **Cognitive behavioral therapy (CBT):** The goal of this treatment is to deal with the ideas, emotions, and behaviors that have emerged from the narcissistic relationship. As a survivor, it gives you the ability to identify and confront anxiety, other interpersonal problems, and self-image issues.

- **Dialectical behavior therapy (DBT):** Together with mindfulness exercises, DBT is used to help patients better control their emotions and build stronger interpersonal bonds.
- **Psychodynamic psychotherapy:** This method focuses on investigating unconscious feelings, ideas, and events in order to better understand the dynamics of toxic relationships and foster growth in oneself.
- **Humanistic psychotherapy:** This therapy strongly emphasizes the role of self-realization and self-acceptance in recovery. It inspires you to investigate your feelings and get a better grasp of who you are.
- **Solution-focused brief therapy (SFBT):** Rather than concentrating on the root of an individual's emotional discomfort, SFBT is a quick, goal-oriented therapy that assists patients in identifying and pursuing specific answers to their issues.
- **Acceptance and commitment therapy (ACT):** This is a mindfulness-based therapeutic approach that assists people in learning to accept their feelings and cultivate the psychological adaptability necessary to make life-improving decisions.

Alternative Techniques for Healing

Consider these healing techniques if you're looking for alternate forms of treatment. For instance, yoga, art therapy, and meditation can support personal development, enhance emotional health, and help you regulate anxiety.

Meditation and mindfulness: Meditating and applying mindfulness to all areas of your life can help you handle stress, contribute to your growth as a person, and improve your overall wellness. Using methods like body scan techniques and breathing exercises can help you become aware of what you're feeling and how your body responds to these emotions. By staying present, you develop a deeper connection with yourself and your surroundings, promoting a sense of calm and balance.

- **Present moment focus:** Mindfulness encourages focusing on the present moment without getting lost in the past or worrying about the future.
- **Guided meditations:** These are meditations that are solely created to help heal your trauma and recover your self-confidence.
- **Stress management and personal growth:** Engaging in meditation and practicing mindfulness in your daily life is like a secret weapon against stress. It contributes to your personal development, helping you become a better version of yourself and enhancing your overall well-being.

Support groups: If you need a safe place to share what you are feeling, what you've been through, and to receive some mental support from others who can relate and have gone through a similar situation, joining a support group is an excellent idea.

Group therapy: This therapy allows you to connect with others who have gone through similar abuse, and you can work together to create methods for coping and, the first prize, healing.

Prayer: If you're spiritual and you connect with a higher force for guidance, it can be supportive of your process of healing.

Emotional detox: Release emotional barricades using the Emotional Freedom Technique (EFT) to encourage recovery.

- **Breaking down emotional barricades:** Emotional detox is like breaking down barriers that have kept your emotions trapped. It's a process of releasing emotional barricades that may have built up over time due to past experiences, especially in a narcissistic relationship.
- **Embracing EFT:** This is a powerful tool in this detox journey. With an emphasis on letting go of negative emotions, EFT incorporates applying gentle pressure on particular areas in your body. It encourages the flow of emotional energy and supports your recovery process.
- **Encouraging recovery and healing:** By employing EFT, you actively participate in your recovery. This technique helps you release emotional burdens, promoting a sense of freedom and contributing to your overall emotional well-being. It's a step in the direction of recovery and mastering your emotions.

Creative expression: Through creative self-expression, art and music therapy assist you in identifying and addressing unpleasant emotions.

Journaling: Jotting down your feelings is a great way to initiate your healing process. It makes it official when you put it to pen and paper. I recommend that you write about what you are experiencing emotionally at least once a day. Also, write about what you are grateful for, even if you can only identify one thing daily.

- **Initiating the healing process:** Journaling acts as a catalyst for your healing. Putting your feelings into words is like giving them a voice, initiating the process of acknowledgment and understanding.
- **Making it official with pen and paper:** The act of physically writing down your thoughts and feelings adds a sense of officiality to your experiences. Pen and paper become your allies in documenting your journey, making it tangible and real.
- **Daily emotional expression:** Make it a habit to write about your emotional experiences at least once a day. This daily practice creates a routine for emotional expression, allowing you to track your progress and gain insights into your emotional landscape.
- **Gratitude journaling for positivity:** In addition to expressing emotions, include a daily list of things you are grateful for. This simple act of gratitude journaling shifts your focus to positive aspects of your life, promoting a more optimistic outlook and fostering emotional well-being.

Somatic therapies: To heal trauma and process feelings Somatic Experiencing and dance/movement therapy places an intense focus on body sensations.

- **Somatic Experiencing:** This is like a friend that helps you heal from tough experiences. Instead of just talking about feelings, it focuses on how your body feels. This method guides you to notice and let go of built-up tension, helping your body slowly deal with challenging events. By paying attention to how your body feels, Somatic Experiencing wants to bring back a feeling of safety and strength.

- **Dance/movement therapy:** Imagine using dance as a way to express how you feel without saying a word. That's what dance/movement therapy does. It lets you show your emotions through movement, giving you a way to deal with tough feelings without talking. By moving mindfully, you can reconnect with your body, let go of bottled-up emotions, and start your journey to feeling better.

Physical practices: Yoga, tai chi, and sound healing can help you grow by managing your tension and upgrading your emotional wellness.

- **Yoga for holistic well-being:** Yoga is known for its holistic approach, addressing both the physical and emotional aspects of well-being. It helps release tension, enhances self-awareness, and fosters emotional balance.
- **Tai chi for mind-body harmony:** Tai chi is a gentle martial art characterized by slow, flowing movements and focused breathwork, fostering a sense of tranquillity Practicing tai chi promotes mind-body harmony, reducing stress and anxiety. It encourages a mindful connection with the body, aiding in emotional regulation and overall well-being.
- **Sound healing for emotional resonance:** Sound healing involves exposure to harmonious sounds and vibrations to promote relaxation and emotional resonance. The therapeutic use of sound, such as singing bowls or calming melodies, can profoundly impact emotional wellness. It helps release tension, enhance mood, and create a harmonious internal environment.

Nature therapy: A sense of grounding and connection with nature can be achieved via forest bathing, vegetable gardening, and the use of pets, which may encourage your healing.

- **Grounding through gardening:** It helps with stress relief and mood-boosting. You can find solace, regain a sense of control, and foster a positive environment for your recovery journey. Gardening offers tangible outcomes, creating a sense of accomplishment. Nurturing plants and witnessing their growth becomes a metaphor for personal healing and resilience, reinforcing one's agency.
- **Create a sacred space:** Designate a garden area as a personal sanctuary for reflection and healing.
- **Mindful Practices:** Engage in gardening mindfully, paying attention to the sensations, smells, and sounds around you.

When it comes to recovering from narcissistic abuse, it is essential to have a strategy and collaborate with a specialist in the area in question. The kind of therapy employed in the treatment of victims of narcissistic abuse may change based on the unique needs and signs experienced by each patient. It's important to investigate your alternatives and choose the best course of action for your unique situation. Recall that the key is discovering what suits you the most and aligns with your inner senses and instincts.

There's Hope in Healing: Choose Your Personal Healing Tribe

When you realize there's a narcissist in your life, what's your next move? How do you begin to heal? For example, if your spouse cheated or walked out on you for someone else, it might hit you with feelings of shame, failure, and weakness. You might even find yourself wanting to isolate from friends and family. While talking openly with your close ones is crucial, it's equally important to trust the right people.

Sometimes, there's someone in your circle causing chaos, spreading gossip, or pretending to take care of you. If this person gossips, it might reach your ex-spouse, causing additional complications. Having such friends or family members can seriously hinder your healing process. It's crucial to distance yourself from anyone negatively impacting your recovery. These individuals tend to drain your energy. Stick with those who genuinely have your back and offer support. Be mindful of who you include in your personal tribe during your healing journey, both in your personal and professional life.

Letting Go of the Rage You Feel to Facilitate Healing

Keeping everything you feel bottled up inside may seem like a safe strategy to protect yourself, but you need to know that somewhere your bottle will blow its top. You need to release some of your emotions before everything blows up all at once.

You may feel angry toward your ex for stealing the best years of your life that you will never be able to get back. If you want to truly heal and move on to a life filled with joy, you need to let go of the anger you are feeling right now. Dealing with these feelings might feel like climbing a sky-high mountain. Well, you will never reach the top if you don't take the first step, will you?

It's time to let out the anger you've been holding back. If you keep it in, it might put your body in constant stress mode, leading to health issues like inflammation because your immune system is focused on dealing with stress. Holding onto this anger could steal away the remaining years of your life.

Getting angry at a narcissist might not be helpful because they thrive on attention, but that doesn't mean you should keep it all to yourself. To start healing, find healthy ways to express your anger. Stop pretending to be okay just to please others.

How do you let go of all those negative feelings? First, recognize what you're feeling. Sometimes, even if you don't feel it, your body is reacting to the emotions you're keeping inside. Here are some good ways to deal with and let out your anger:

- Get moving physically, like dancing or exercising, to let go of that angry energy. Do physical activities that help release aggression, like using a punching bag or playing sports. Take a walk or do some intense exercise to shift your focus and release pent-up anger.
- When you go jogging, use noise-canceling headphones or find different routes to avoid things that trigger your anger, like loud noises or stressful commutes.
- Try calming techniques, such as deep breathing, to help relax your nerves and dial down the anger.
- Write in a journal to express your feelings in a positive way and work through them.
- Practice meditation or yoga to feel more peaceful and let go of built-up aggression.
- Skip alcohol when you're upset; it can make emotions worse and mess with your ability to handle anger.

Remember, it's okay to feel angry, but find healthy ways, like these, to let it out.

BREAKOUT BOX: UNLOCKING YOUR HEALING JOURNEY

After experiencing narcissistic abuse, recovering from it takes fortitude and introspection. This is your manual for releasing your bonds and nourishing your soul:

- **Recognize the deep scars:** Understand the traumatic reactions like freezing, fleeing, fighting, or fawning that may linger after a narcissistic relationship. Acknowledge the emotional wounds to start your healing journey.
- **Move on with purpose:** Break free from the shackles of a narcissistic relationship. Prioritize your emotional health by leaving toxic environments, rebuilding self-esteem, and reclaiming control over your life.
- **Navigate emotional scars:** Grapple with long-lasting effects on your emotions—battered and drained, traumatized, and struggling with guilt and insecurity. Understand the challenges but remember, healing is possible.
- **Prioritize emotional health:** Eva's story teaches us the importance of prioritizing emotional health. Co-parenting, learning to live independently, and prioritizing well-being are crucial steps in breaking free.
- **Nourish your spirit:** Explore therapeutic techniques like CBT, DBT, psychodynamic psychotherapy, humanistic psychotherapy, SFBT, ACT, and EMDR. These can aid in understanding, confronting, and overcoming the aftermath of narcissistic abuse.
- **Alternative healing methods:** Embrace alternative forms of therapy such as meditation, support groups, group therapy, prayer, emotional detox, creative therapies, journaling, somatic therapies, physical practices, and nature

therapy. These can promote personal growth and emotional wellness.

It would help to accept that healing is an ongoing personalized journey, not your end destination. It's not linear, and that's okay! Collaborate with specialists, experiment with various methods, and discover what resonates with your inner self. The key lies in finding what suits you best and aligns with your instincts. Your healing journey is unique, and every step forward is a victory.

———

As you embark on the next chapter of your healing journey, it's crucial to realize that the scars of a narcissistic relationship don't define you. Chapter 3, titled "You're More Than What They Made You Feel," delves into the process of reclaiming your identity and rediscovering your worth. Let this chapter serve as a guiding light, enabling you to break free from the shadows of self-doubt and emerge stronger than ever. It's time to rewrite the narrative someone else imposed on you and embrace the truth—you are resilient, you are valuable, and you are more than what they made you feel. Let's talk about how to create a life that is authentically and unapologetically yours.

3. You're More Than What They Made You Feel

During her marriage to Tom, a colleague and photographer, Hannah, a once-confident journalist, faced a decline in her self-esteem. Tom's initial criticism focused on Hannah's work: her articles and reporting style. Over time, Tom's criticism became more personal, targeting Hannah's character, her level of intelligence, and even her appearance.

These constant negative remarks eroded Hannah's self-worth, making her question her abilities as a journalist and, worse, her value as a person. Hannah knew she had to leave the relationship, it was the only way to find herself again.

Post-divorce, Hannah received an important assignment to cover a major news event abroad. The assignment placed her in a new environment, away from Tom's shadow and his hurtful words. She interacted with international colleagues who were unaware of her personal struggles and admired her journalistic abilities.

The thrill of this assignment and the positive feedback she received helped Hannah feel more confident and rediscover her passion for journalism. This experience abroad was a turning point, reminding Hannah of her talent, skill, and worth.

In the next part, we're going to discuss the process of building back your confidence and feeling good about yourself. This chapter is like a roadmap, giving you practical tips and strong strategies to feel better about who you are. Come along as we figure out how to rediscover your true self and realize that you're much more than what others may have made you believe.

STEP 3—(E)LEVATE YOUR SELF-WORTH

Self-worth is essential as it lays the groundwork for our emotional well-being and mental health. It plays a vital role in fostering healthy relationships, enabling us to set boundaries and choose respectful connections. A strong sense of self-worth acts as a resilience buffer against life's challenges, motivating us to pursue goals and navigate setbacks. It is closely linked to good mental health, reducing the likelihood of anxiety and depression. Moreover, self-worth positively influences decision-making, communication, and emotional regulation, contributing to overall life satisfaction and happiness. Our self-worth shapes our identity, influencing how we perceive ourselves and interact with the world.

The Slow Fading of Your Self-Worth

Being in a relationship with a narcissist can really mess with how you feel about yourself. They use all sorts of tactics to make you doubt your worth and abilities, like making mean comments, messing with your head (called gaslighting), and criticizing everything from how you look to what you achieve. They might even embarrass you in front of others or use sarcasm to put you down. By playing mind games, a narcissist slowly breaks down how you see yourself until you start believing the negative things they say. This constant undervaluing can mess with your emotions and how you see yourself for a long time. Dealing with a narcissist is super harmful, and getting out of that situation as soon as you can is often the best way to start healing in the long run.

When you come out of an abusive relationship you may feel anxious, depressed, and in such a low, low place. Many women find themselves at rock bottom, with little to no money, and having to start from scratch. At this time, you may blame yourself for being so stupid to have stayed in the relationship for so long or for not seeing the signs. Being extremely self-critical is also part of your healing journey. However, excessive guilt and shame can affect your self-worth greatly and place you in a "freeze" state of mind. It would be best to deal with it immediately so it does not stop you from going on with your life.

Mirror, Mirror: How Narcissists Distort Your Self-Image

Narcissists employ a multitude of manipulative techniques to alter their partner's self-perception. A few of them (but as I said, there are many more) include gaslighting, love bombing, guilt-tripping, and lying. Let's discuss these and some other tactics (Gillis, 2022; Craft, 2022; Abuse Warrior, n.d):

- **Gaslighting:** Narcissists often use this sneaky move to mess with your head. They twist the truth or make things up to make you doubt what you know is real. Gaslighting can really mess with your confidence and make you feel like you're not worth much. It's a tricky tactic that messes with your sense of reality and can leave you feeling pretty down about yourself. Picture this scenario: Your partner consistently talks about a new friend from work, subtly highlighting shared activities. This deliberate vagueness sparks jealousy and competition, making you question your relationship's stability and your own worth in comparison. This is triangulation in action—an insidious tactic used by narcissists to manipulate emotions and create discord.

- **Love bombing:** This tactic is when someone showers you with loads of affection and attention to make you feel super special. But watch out because behind all that lovey-dovey stuff, there's often a hidden agenda. It's like they're trying to make you rely on them completely and have control over you. So, while it might feel amazing initially, it's important to be aware that it can be a tactic to gain influence and power in the relationship. Picture a new romantic interest overwhelming you with constant affection, compliments, and attention. However, beneath this charming exterior lies a hidden agenda—aiming to foster dependence and gain control. Initially enticing, the love bombing tactic ultimately serves as a manipulative strategy to wield influence in the relationship.

- **Guilt-tripping:** This tactic is when a narcissist tries to make you feel responsible for stuff, even if it's not really you. They use this sneaky tactic to control how you think and make you do what they want. It's like they lay on the blame to manipulate your feelings and actions, keeping you under their influence. It's not fair and can really mess with your head and emotions. Here's an example: "I always go out of my way to make you happy, but it seems like you never appreciate it. I sacrifice so much for you, and this is how you repay me?"

- **Messing with the truth:** Narcissists often resort to lying to trick and manipulate their partner, all for their own benefit. They make up stuff to control the situation and get what they want. Deception becomes their go-to move to keep things in their favor. So, if you catch them spinning a web of lies, it's a sign they're trying to play games with you for their personal gain. For example, your partner frequently claims to be at work when, in fact, they're spending time somewhere else.
- **Projection:** Projection is when someone blames you for things they do themselves. It can make you feel inferior, unworthy, and at fault. Here's an example: They accuse you of being overly controlling when, in reality, they are the one who exhibits controlling behavior.
- **Negging:** This tactic is when someone gives you compliments that actually criticize you, making you doubt yourself. It leaves you feeling inadequate and full of self-doubt. For example, "You're so smart for someone who didn't attend college."
- **Triangulation:** Triangulation is when someone brings in another person to create jealousy or competition, resulting in betrayal, mistrust, and bamboozlement. For example, a narcissistic partner might intentionally become overly friendly with an ex-partner or a colleague, fueling speculation and insecurity. This calculated maneuver aims to instigate a sense of rivalry, making you question your worth and the stability of your relationship. Triangulation is a toxic game, leaving you in a web of emotional turmoil and fractured trust.
- **Withholding affection/attention:** A narcissist might purposefully not show love or attention to make you anxious. This tactic leads to feelings of rejection, insecurity, and emotional distress. For example, they might ignore your

attempts at physical affection or emotional connection as a form of punishment.

- **Silent treatment:** Ignoring you to make you question what you did wrong and as a result causing isolation, frustration, and emotional distress. For example, your partner refusing to speak to you for an extended period after a disagreement leaves you feeling uncertain and distressed.

- **Shifting goalposts:** This tactic involves changing expectations so you always feel like you're falling short. It results in frustration, confusion, and self-doubt. For example, your partner was constantly changing expectations in your relationship, which made it impossible for you to meet their ever-shifting standards.

- **Isolation:** Isolation occurs when someone cuts you off from friends and family to have ultimate power over you. It leads to loneliness, isolation, and emotional distress. For example, a narcissist might discourage you from spending time with your loved ones, creating a situation where they are the sole source of support.

- **Blame shifting:** Never taking responsibility and blaming you for everything is a tactic called blame shifting. It makes you feel guilty, embarrassed, and critical of yourself. Here's an example: "You made me so angry that I couldn't help but react that way. It's your fault for pushing me."

- **Playing on insecurities:** A narcissist might exploit your flaws to make you feel like you're not good enough. This behavior results in self-doubt, low self-esteem, and emotional distress. For example, your partner might exploit your fear of abandonment by threatening to leave whenever there's a disagreement.

- **Invalidation:** Invalidation involves dismissing your feelings as irrational or unimportant. It leads to emotional invalidation, self-doubt, and emotional distress. For example, someone might dismiss your emotions by saying, "You're overreacting. It's not a big deal, and you're being too sensitive."

These tactics work to erode the victim's sense of self and diminish their social standing in an effort to dominate and control. It's important for victims in such relationships to recognize these manipulation tactics and seek support to protect themselves from further harm. After enduring such extreme forms of manipulation, you may find it challenging to trust your perception and thoughts as well as make your own decisions.

Rebuilding From the Ground Up

Getting back your confidence and rediscovering who you are after dealing with narcissistic abuse is hard, but it's super important. Here are several useful methods to assist you through this process:

- **Let your feelings out:** Give yourself permission to experience and deal with the emotions that were pushed down during the abusive relationship. This strategy can reconnect you with your genuine self and support emotional recovery.
- **Get back in touch with who you were before the abuse:** Make amends with the person you used to be, and forgive yourself for letting the abusive relationship affect you. Doing this step is important for finding peace with your past and rediscovering your value as a person.

- **Identify your strengths:** Take note of your positive qualities and skills that may have been overlooked during the abusive relationship (Akin, 2022). Identifying your strengths can contribute to rebuilding your self-confidence and self-assurance.
- **Cultivate positive connections:** Surround yourself with people who are supportive and understanding. Form connections with people who genuinely value and respect you (Akin, 2022). Building healthy relationships can enhance your sense of belonging and self-worth.
- **Be good to yourself:** Show yourself kindness by being understanding and using positive affirmations daily. This strategy helps push back against self-criticism and negative thoughts about yourself (Akin, 2022). Being kind to yourself is crucial for boosting your self-esteem and learning to accept who you are.
- **Learn to decline:** Set and uphold boundaries to safeguard your well-being and prioritize what you need and want (Jack, 2020; Akin, 2022). Creating healthy boundaries is essential for reclaiming control and maintaining self-respect.
- **Enhance your mental and physical well-being:** Pay attention to self-care, participate in activities that boost your overall health, and seek professional help (Akin, 2022). Making your mental and physical health a priority contributes to a positive self-perception and self-value.
- **Simplify your understanding of your feelings and thoughts:** Engage in mindfulness and self-reflection to comprehend and handle how the abuse has affected your mental and emotional health (Akin, 2022). Developing self-awareness plays a crucial role in reconstructing self-esteem and a solid sense of self.

- **Realize it was never your fault:** Acknowledge that the abuse wasn't your fault and free yourself from self-blame and guilt (Akin, 2022). Transferring the responsibility from yourself to the abuser is vital for rebuilding your self-worth and self-compassion.
- **Adopt a mindset focused on growth:** Stay open to learning, adapting, and reshaping your identity following the abuse (Akin, 2022). Embracing personal growth and self-discovery is crucial for regaining a strong sense of self.

Reconstructing self-esteem and your sense of self after narcissistic abuse is a gradual and continuous journey that demands patience, self-compassion, and support. Consulting with therapists or counselors can offer valuable guidance and assistance during this healing process.

Taking Your Self-Care Seriously

Have you noticed how you are always trying to help others and make sure they are okay to make yourself feel better? It's okay to do good for your children, family, and friends, but it should not be at your own cost. You may be placing yourself right at the bottom of the self-care food chain. Be careful when you do this because you might starve yourself. And then, you won't be able to feed anyone else.

You may take care of your physical health but forget about your emotional and psychological health, or vice versa. You need to place your health high on your priority list but follow a holistic approach to your self-healing through nutrition, hydration, sleep, exercise, mental health, and emotional wellness strategies.

Face it, not all of us have the money or time to go on a spa week retreat, but don't fret. It doesn't mean you can't take care of yourself. There are small actions you can do consistently to make yourself feel more rested, healthier, and happier.

What exactly are you doing for you over the next seven days? Even if you take ten minutes daily, write it down in your journal, and commit to it. It can be anything, even a toilet break behind a closed door without your children for five minutes daily, but at least try to go out if you can. You can go for a walk, take your coffee outside barefoot in sunlight, do a quick meditation, or take a relaxing bath. Your inner child is crying out for your attention. Why are you only prioritizing your external children, but neglecting your inner child to feel not good enough or worthy of your time? Book some time to spend with your inner child daily.

Role-model self-love to your children. Do you want them to be stressed and burnt-out adults? No, you won't want that at all. So show them that you take care of yourself, and they will create a positive picture of self-care in their minds for the future.

Rerouting Yourself in the Correct Direction

Because of the time spent with a narcissist, your self-worth was probably directed out of the side door.

Your self-worth plays a big role in how you navigate life. Even if you try to hide it, your energy level, or "vibration," is something people can sense, whether they're aware of it or not. Concealing your feelings well might seem like a skill, but it can be detrimental because it reduces the chance of someone noticing and offering support.

I've observed a lot, and it's tough to see people with a slower, dull energy struggling. I want to remind everyone: You matter! You exist, and that's enough. It's not always easy, though, for various reasons.

When recovering from narcissistic abuse, your energy may be lower, so it's essential to guide yourself back in a positive direction. Here are six tips on how to reroute your self-worth in the right direction:

- **Conditional or unconditional:** Reflect on whether your self-worth depends on external factors or is unconditional. If it relies on being above average or others' opinions, it's conditional. Focus on feeling your own love and respect yourself unconditionally.
- **Don't compete and compare:** Don't base your self-worth on physical achievements. Comparing yourself to others can lead to challenges. Your value isn't about what you do; it's about who you are inherently.
- **Stop your inner voice from creating fear:** If you've experienced narcissistic influence, negative thoughts and self-doubt can be overwhelming. Stop the inner dialogue and focus on living in the present. Your true nature is constant, clouded by the mind's noise.
- **Pinpoint your main values to live by:** Identify your core values—kindness, compassion, empathy—and establish principles like honesty. Don't prioritize pleasing others. Your value comes from internal measures you've set for yourself.
- **Walk this Earth with thanks:** What you focus on in life grows. Acknowledge both happiness and unhappiness. Count your blessings, reflect on what you're proud of or what you've learned. Move your focus to positive things about your life.
- **Have empathy toward yourself:** Monitor how you talk to yourself. Challenge negative inner voices and commit to being more positive and respectful. You are good enough to receive empathy and kindness from yourself.

You are worth it!

BREAKOUT BOX: REDISCOVERING YOUR WORTH

Remember, you are more than the sum of your past experiences.

Hannah travelled halfway across the world to get her self-worth back. She was already good enough, she just failed to realize it. We can learn a lot from Hannah. Taking a proactive approach early in your journey to know exactly who you are and celebrate it is crucial. Also, you need to ensure that you have the right support system right here where you are to have your back when feelings of uncertainty and unworthiness plague you.

- **Acknowledge your resilience:** Recognize the strength it took to endure and break free from a narcissistic relationship. Your resilience is a testimony of your innermost power—acknowledge and celebrate it.
- **Embrace your uniqueness:** Your identity is not defined by the scars of the past. Embrace your uniqueness and the qualities that make you authentically you. Shift the focus from what was taken to what remains and flourishes within you.
- **Learn from the pain:** Every painful experience is an opportunity for growth. Reflect on the lessons learned during the journey of starting your life from scratch. Transform adversity into a catalyst for personal development and wisdom.
- **Set boundaries with self-compassion:** Establish healthy boundaries, not only with others but also with yourself. Practice self-compassion by acknowledging your needs and honoring your emotions without judgment.

- **Celebrate small victories:** Break down the monumental task of rebuilding into small, achievable goals. Celebrate each victory, no matter how minor, as a step toward reclaiming your self-worth.
- **Surround yourself with support:** Cultivate a support network of understanding friends, family, or professionals. Share your journey and allow others to uplift and affirm your value.
- **Take part in self-discovery exercises:** Rekindle your passions and hobbies that have perhaps faded. Take part in things that give you a sense of direction and make you happy and fulfilled.
- **Challenge negative self-talk:** Identify and challenge the negative thoughts implanted by the narcissistic relationship. Replace self-deprecating thoughts with affirmations that reinforce your worth.

Remember, the process of rebuilding has its ups and downs. You are on the path to rediscovering your worth, and each step forward is a triumph in reclaiming the authentic and resilient person you are.

———

As we venture into the next chapter, "It's Okay to Say No," the focus shifts toward empowering boundaries and reclaiming control over your own life story. "No" is not just a word; it's your declaration of self-respect. In a world where the echoes of narcissistic relationships may linger, learning to set boundaries becomes a cornerstone of self-preservation. Join me as we unravel the importance of saying no, and how this seemingly simple word can be a transformative tool in your journey toward healing.

4. It's Okay to Say No

Sophia was initially drawn to Ethan's decisiveness, finding his take-charge attitude attractive. However, things took a turn after they got married. Ethan's controlling behavior went beyond making decisions; he started telling Sophia how to dress, monitoring her friendships, and making unwelcome comments about her weight. Sophia felt like she was losing herself and constantly doubting her choices. This emotional toll made her once-vibrant personality fade, which left her feeling alone.

Even after their divorce, Ethan's need for control persisted. He bombarded Sophia with calls, offering unsolicited advice about her career and personal life. Recognizing the need for boundaries, Sophia took action: she blocked Ethan during work hours, set clear communication rules, and sought therapy to rebuild her self-worth. Over time, Ethan's attempts to control her lessened as Sophia established firm boundaries. Her journey became one of rediscovery, as she not only set limits with Ethan but also reconnected with her passions, experiencing a newfound sense of freedom she hadn't felt in years.

In this chapter, we concentrate on the value of establishing boundaries. After reading this chapter, you will be well-equipped for setting and maintaining firm boundaries.

Step 4—(E)mpower Through Boundaries

Setting boundaries with a narcissist can feel like navigating an uphill battle due to the inherent challenges posed by their behavior. Narcissists, by nature, have a persistent desire to exercise authority and power. They often view boundaries as threats to their authority and manipulate situations to test and push against established limits.

In relationships with narcissists, the constant testing of boundaries manifests in various ways. They may disregard personal space, invade privacy, or dismiss any attempt to establish limits. Narcissists thrive on asserting power, and the more they sense resistance, the more determined they become to break down those boundaries. This relentless push can leave you feeling overwhelmed and trapped in a dynamic where asserting personal limits is met with resistance, manipulation, or even aggression. Understanding this dynamic is crucial for anyone seeking to establish and maintain boundaries in a relationship with a narcissist. But what if the relationship is over?

You see, after being used to giving in to a narcissist's demands for too long, you may not have the skills to say no or set any form of boundary in your personal or work life anymore. It's not all lost. You must retrain your brain by creating and repeating new behaviors.

Why Do Narcissists Hate Boundaries?

Narcissistic abuse is a form of abuse that violates your boundaries in the worst way (because it's subtle). Narcissistic abusers don't want it to appear that they're overstepping your boundaries, so they operate cleverly so that you are mostly unaware that your boundaries are being violated.

Narcissists really don't like boundaries, and there are a few reasons why that's the case:

- **Narcissists want to be in control all the time.** They believe they are superior to others and should be given a higher priority. When someone else sets boundaries, it messes with their control and makes them feel less powerful, and that's something they can't handle.
- **Despite acting all high and mighty, narcissists actually have pretty delicate self-esteem.** They constantly need praise and admiration to feel good about themselves. So when you set boundaries, they might take it as a personal hit, feeling rejected or criticized, making them defensive.
- **Narcissists aren't great at understanding or respecting other people's needs and boundaries.** They see relationships as opportunities for their personal benefit and might ignore or dismiss what others want.
- **Narcissists think they own the right to priority treatment and exceptions.** So, when others set boundaries, it feels like they're being mistreated, going against their belief that they should have unlimited access to everything they want.
- **Deep down, narcissists are scared of being left alone or rejected.** That's why they constantly seek attention and validation. Boundaries make them worry about being left out or rejected, making them really not like the idea of boundaries.
- **On top of these, narcissists also avoid boundaries because they prefer being super close with others, feel entitled, and don't like hearing "no."** Trying to set and

stick to boundaries with a narcissist can be challenging; they might get mad or try to manipulate the situation because it challenges their need for control and their belief that they're better than everyone else.

Knowing these reasons can help you handle relationships with narcissists and make sure you're looking out for yourself.

Signs That Your Boundaries Are Being Violated

Do you justify someone else's behavior and make excuses for it? When things don't work out, do you place the responsibility on yourself? Are you starting to doubt your decisions and just going along with things without fighting back to keep the peace? Are you doubting your ability to protect yourself? Are you unsure about who you are? Are you sacrificing yourself and losing your sanity? You sense something is off, but you can't really pin it down. You now realize that someone is crossing your limits; that's what's wrong.

If you try to make a decision or set a boundary, a narcissist may ignore you. This is because they want to test your limits and see what they can get away with.

Let's walk through some indicators that your boundaries are being crossed.

- **Physical symptoms:** You can develop physical symptoms such as headaches, stomach aches, or insomnia due to the stress and anxiety that the narcissist's boundary violations are causing.
- **Feeling overwhelmed:** You constantly feel overwhelmed by the demands and expectations of others, unable to manage your own priorities.

- **Ignoring your feelings:** When others consistently dismiss or ignore your feelings, it leaves you feeling invalidated or unheard.
- **Constant criticism:** When you experience frequent criticism that erodes your self-esteem, it can leave you questioning your worth and capabilities.
- **Manipulation tactics:** The narcissist can use manipulative tactics to make you doubt your perceptions, emotions, or even your memories.
- **Invasion of personal space:** When you feel that your personal space is invaded physically, emotionally, or digitally, it can cause discomfort and unease.
- **Excessive demands:** The narcissist will let you face unreasonable or excessive demands, influencing your time, energy, or resources without any consideration for your well-being.
- **Pressure to conform:** You may experience pressure to conform to someone else's expectations or values, leaving little room for your individuality.
- **Consistent disregard for consent:** You may experience situations where your boundaries are consistently disregarded, especially in areas involving personal choices or physical touch.
- **Isolation from others:** The narcissist may do things to isolate you from friends, family, or support networks, creating dependence on the person violating your boundaries.
- **Unwarranted control:** They may be exerting unwarranted control over aspects of your life, restricting your autonomy and decision-making.
- **Constant apologizing:** You find yourself apologizing excessively, even when you haven't done anything wrong, to maintain harmony or avoid conflict.

- **Gaslighting:** You are encountering gaslighting behavior where your reality is questioned, causing confusion and self-doubt.
- **Lack of support:** You don't receive any support from the narcissist when you express your needs or concerns. This makes you feel isolated and alone in your struggles.
- **Persistent disrespect:** You are facing consistent disrespect for your values, beliefs, or opinions by the narcissist. This makes you question the relationship's sincerity.

Recognizing these signs is crucial for keeping healthy boundaries and taking steps to address any violations that may be occurring in your relationships.

Setting Boundaries With the Master Manipulator

Setting boundaries with a narcissist can be extremely challenging due to their inherent traits and psychological makeup. When attempting to set boundaries with a narcissist, individuals may encounter various obstacles, including pushback, anger, manipulation, and a lack of respect for the established limits.

Keep your feelings and responses at bay during exchanges with them. Try the gray rock technique—it's like talking to a rock and showing no emotions, especially when dealing with narcissists. They feed off your reactions, wanting to see you upset or under their control. Set a personal boundary first to know when someone is crossing the line.

To make things easier, keep your communication straightforward. Here are three simple strategies you can use right away:

- **Be boring:** Keep your responses short and your personal information and feelings private.
- **Stay calm:** Don't react when they try to enrage you or start a fight.
- **Stick to your plan:** Keep using these tactics constantly, so they know you're not giving them any emotional drama.

Remember, it's okay to walk away if you're being disrespected. You don't owe anyone anything. Clearly state your boundaries, and make it clear what the consequences will be if they're crossed. Stick to your word, and don't make hollow threats. Your boundaries are your own business; you don't need to explain them to anyone. Focus on yourself, practice self-care, and show love and respect for yourself.

Boundaries are like a nightmare for narcissists; they may become more hostile and abusive when you establish them. But know that they're working because you're taking away their power to disrespect you. Heal yourself and become a strong individual to protect yourself. If you carry yourself seriously, they will view you this way, too. Know your values, what you won't tolerate, and when it's time to walk away.

Challenges When Setting Boundaries With a Narcissist

Here are some specific challenges faced when setting boundaries with a narcissist, along with solutions to overcome them:

- **Facing resistance and anger:** When you try to set boundaries with a narcissist, expect them to resist. They might get mad, try to control you more, manipulate you, or ignore your boundaries (Grande, 2023).

- **What you can do:** Get help from your loved ones. Having people who understand your situation can boost your confidence when the narcissist pushes back.
- **Disregard for boundaries:** Narcissists usually don't care about other people's boundaries. They might ignore or dismiss what you've set (Grande, 2023).
- **What you can do:** Be crystal clear and firm about your boundaries. Stay consistent in sticking to them, and don't back down.
- **Narcissistic rage:** Some narcissists react with intense anger when confronted with boundaries, making the situation tough emotionally (Grande, 2023).
- **What you can do:** Have a plan to leave if things get unsafe emotionally or physically. It's crucial to know how to remove yourself from a harmful situation.
- **Manipulative tricks:** Narcissists might use manipulation to break down your boundaries and regain control (Anwar, 2022).
- **What you can do:** Don't get involved in emotional drama or try to explain your boundaries. Keep your focus on your well-being and the importance of keeping healthy limits.
- **Fear of abandonment:** Narcissists often fear rejection and being left alone, driving their constant need for attention. Boundaries can trigger this fear, making them strongly against it (Empathic Warrior, 2023).
- **What you can do:** Stick to your boundaries and seek support to manage any guilt or obligation you might feel.

It's crucial to set and communicate boundaries effectively. This involves understanding narcissistic personalities, knowing your limits, communicating assertively, and setting consequences that make sense and can be consistently enforced. By recognizing these challenges and using effective strategies, you can work toward establishing and maintaining healthy boundaries when dealing with a narcissist.

Why Would Narcissists Want to Test Your Boundaries?

Narcissists push and test boundaries for different reasons, all tied to their personalities and how they think. Here's why they do it:

- **Thinking they're better:** Narcissists believe they're above rules and limits. Pushing boundaries is their way of showing they're in charge and don't like being restricted.
- **Not caring about others:** Since they lack empathy, narcissists ignore what others need. They feel they deserve special treatment and push boundaries to get what they want, not thinking about how it affects others.
- **Controlling others:** Testing boundaries helps narcissists see how much control they have. They do it to manipulate and dominate people, proving to themselves how powerful they are.
- **Needing attention:** By pushing limits, narcissists see how much attention and admiration they can get. They do it to ensure they get the praise and attention they need.
- **Avoiding rejection:** Narcissists fear being rejected or criticized. Pushing boundaries helps them avoid feeling rejected and challenges any criticism they might face.
- **Finding it fun:** Some narcissists enjoy causing discomfort or confusion by pushing boundaries. It's like entertainment for them to see how others react.
- **Avoiding responsibility:** Ignoring boundaries lets narcissists dodge responsibility for what they do. They push limits to escape consequences or blame others.
- **Avoiding abandonment:** Narcissists push boundaries to stay in control and avoid being left alone. They're scared of

losing the attention they get, so they push limits to keep that from happening.

Sometimes, people have weak or even no boundaries at all for different reasons, like growing up in an unstable environment or fearing conflict and rejection. Knowing why narcissists act this way helps you understand and deal with these behaviors in your relationships. Setting and sticking to healthy boundaries is crucial to protect your well-being when dealing with narcissists and people in general.

Why Boundaries Matter: More Than Just Lines in the Sand

Boundaries matter in relationships because of their role in maintaining one's mental and emotional well-being and, ultimately, in one's identity. Here are reasons why you need boundaries:

- **Setting boundaries is like creating rules for how you want to be treated.** This guarantees that your interactions are appropriate, kind, and courteous. It's like having a guide for how people should behave around you.
- **Healthy communication is about recognizing and talking about what you need and believe in.** This helps build trust and understanding in your relationships, both with yourself and with others.
- **Think of boundaries as personal space protectors.** They keep your physical, emotional, and mental space safe, so you can keep some things private and make decisions for yourself in your relationships.
- **Having boundaries is like having a stress-relief button.** They help keep your relationships positive, reduce stress, and keep you feeling good overall.

- **Setting limits is also helpful in maintaining your integrity.** They keep you from losing sight of who you are and what you believe in, so you can be an active part of your own life instead of just going along with what others want.
- **Taking charge of your boundaries is like taking control of your personal growth.** It makes you feel more in control, boosts your confidence, and helps you grow as a person.
- **On the safety front, boundaries are like a shield.** They protect you from being taken advantage of, getting hurt, or feeling drained emotionally. Setting and sticking to healthy boundaries lets you focus on what you need and keeps your mental and emotional well-being safe.

So why do boundaries matter in relationships? They create guidelines for respect, protect your personal space, help communication, reduce stress, boost personal growth, prevent harm, and keep you true to yourself. Having and keeping these healthy boundaries ensures your relationships are filled with respect, appropriateness, and care, which is good for your well-being.

Interactive Breakout Box: Navigating Boundaries With Narcissists

Boundaries are a reflection of your self-respect.

Setting boundaries is about respecting yourself. Handling the challenges of narcissists and their struggles with boundaries requires a smart and proactive approach. As we saw in Sophia's case, even after their divorce, a narcissist's control can continue, and it's necessary to take action and implement boundaries. Check out this user-friendly guide to help you navigate this tricky situation:

- **State your boundaries as clearly as possible:** Speak up and be clear when letting the narcissist know your limits. Use strong, assertive language to make sure your boundaries are crystal clear.
- **Know when to say "no":** Identify situations where saying "no" is crucial. Trust your gut and prioritize your well-being instead of always giving in to the narcissist's demands.
- **Practice assertive communication:** Use assertive communication to effectively convey your boundaries. Be confident, straightforward, and direct when expressing what you're comfortable with.
- **Handle your emotions:** Develop strategies to handle your emotions when facing pushback. Stay calm and collected, and don't let emotional manipulation change your stance.
- **Set fair consequences:** Establish consequences for crossing your boundaries that are fair and can be consistently enforced. This helps emphasize the importance of respecting your limits.
- **Get help from others:** Build your tribe. Talk to family or friends for encouragement. Having people in your corner can boost your confidence in sticking to your boundaries.

Remember, boundaries show self-respect. By using these strategies, you can navigate the challenges of dealing with narcissists in your relationships while safeguarding your emotional well-being.

———

The next chapter, "Preparing for Battle, but Hoping for Peace," builds on the theme of setting boundaries with narcissists. This chapter will explore the concept of being proactive and vigilant in the face of challenging relationships while still striving for harmony and emotional well-being. The phrase "Si vis pacem, para bellum" (If you want peace, prepare for war) encapsulates the paradox of preparing for potential conflict while desiring tranquility.

We will discuss actionable strategies for maintaining resilience and emotional balance, akin to preparing for battle while holding onto the hope for peaceful resolutions in the midst of challenging dynamics. This chapter aims to empower individuals to navigate complex relationships with a sense of preparedness, while still fostering optimism for positive outcomes.

5. Preparing for Battle, but Hoping for Peace

Carlos and Nina, once deeply in love, saw their marriage fall apart over time. The divorce turned into a tough battle over their assets and finances. Nina, who seemed charming on the surface, had a manipulative side that few knew about.

As they went through the divorce, Nina tried to hide assets and drain their joint account. She secretly moved money around and sold their shared property without Carlos knowing. Carlos, initially trusting, only realized the extent of Nina's cunning nature once it was too late.

Feeling overwhelmed and realizing he needed help, Carlos turned to close friends for advice. Following their suggestions, he hired a specialized attorney known for handling tricky and contentious divorce cases. Together, Carlos and his attorney meticulously gathered evidence, tracked down hidden transactions, and built a strong case against Nina's deceitful actions.

STEP 5—(D)ETERMINE YOUR LEGAL STRATEGY

Why It's Not Just Another Divorce

Divorcing someone with narcissistic traits can be really tough. Unlike a regular divorce, dealing with a narcissist requires extra caution and preparation. They often play mind games, like refusing to share financial records, not cooperating with you or your lawyer, being mean or vengeful, blaming others, and ignoring court orders. When navigating this process, it's crucial to document everything, including texts and emails.

Narcissists hate compromising, so these divorces often end up in court. Working with a lawyer who understands these challenges is key to protecting yourself. It's also smart to gather supportive people around you and, if possible, avoid direct face-to-face interactions with the narcissistic ex, especially when it comes to parenting.

In the Courtroom With a Puppeteer

Narcissists use tricky tactics in legal situations, especially during divorce. They might try to delay things, act like the victim, intimidate, manipulate evidence, lie in court, emotionally manipulate, demand a lot of money for legal fees, hide money, use kids against you, ruin your reputation, drown you in paperwork, and refuse to talk. These tactics can really mess with your mind, wallet, and emotions, affecting you and your kids if you are a parent.

Knowing these tactics and recognizing the signs is crucial to plan a successful divorce. Getting support from a mental health professional and hiring a savvy divorce lawyer is a must—they'll guide and protect you. Being aware of what you might face helps you feel more in control and ready to handle the challenges of divorcing a narcissist.

It's crucial to distance yourself emotionally and get help from a mental health expert to deal with the emotional toll of your divorce. Concentrate on things you can handle and gather proof to back up your side—this makes you feel more in charge. Knowing what you might face helps you plan and be ready for a successful resolution in your divorce.

Sneaky Tactics in Divorce

- **Dragging things out:** Narcissists can intentionally slow down the divorce process, causing emotional and financial stress for the other person. They might "lose" important documents, request delays, or avoid settling agreements.
- **Playing the victim:** Narcissists are good at painting themselves as victims to get sympathy and weaken their ex-partner's position. This act is a way for them to control and sway the divorce outcome.
- **Intimidation and threats:** Using intimidation and threats, narcissists aim to control the situation. This behavior could involve verbal, emotional, or even physical intimidation to instill fear in the other person.
- **Twisting the truth:** Narcissists might manipulate evidence to support their side or discredit their ex-partner. This tactic could involve using various forms of communication or creating false stories.
- **Lying under oath:** Some narcissists go as far as lying under oath to manipulate the legal process. This is a serious offense and goes against the legal system.
- **Messing with emotions:** Emotional manipulation is a common tool for narcissists to control their ex-partner's emotions and actions. This can have a significant impact on the victim's mental well-being.

- **Draining finances:** Narcissists may demand excessive legal fees to drain the resources of their ex-partner, making it hard for them to continue the divorce process.
- **Scheming about finances:** Financial manipulation includes hiding assets or providing false financial information to influence settlements and maintain control even after the divorce. They will lie about their income, lie about their job, or even quit their job to get financial support from you. You need to document everything you need to know about them.
- **Using kids as tools:** Narcissists might try to get full custody or limit the other person's access to the kids, not necessarily for the children's sake but to hurt their ex-partner. They may also use the kids as their excuse to get financial gain.
- **Ruining reputations:** Character assassination involves spreading false accusations about the other person to damage their reputation in court. The narcissist's pain can drive them to do and say irrational things that are really out of line with reality. They will bad-mouth you with other people involved in the case. That's why you need to document everything that happens to keep your side of the story fact-based and clear.
- **Paperwork overload:** Flooding the other party with paperwork is a tactic to drain their resources and make the divorce process more expensive and challenging.
- **Silent treatment:** By refusing to communicate or mediate, narcissists force the other person to deal only through lawyers, adding to the cost and time of the divorce.

These tactics can seriously affect the victim's mental health, financial stability, and the overall divorce process. It's crucial for you to be aware of these tricks and seek support in navigating these challenges.

The Impact of the Narcissist's Divorce Tactics

I found myself bumping into many people who suffered at the hands of a narcissist, in particular, without knowing it. Actually, during the divorce process, it seemed to me that people weren't sure when they were in the relationship, and they really only came to understand that, in fact, they had been in an abusive relationship with a narcissist for many years when they were already separated or busy with the divorce process.

The above-mentioned divorce tactics extend beyond the legal battle. They can have a severe psychological and financial impact on you, especially when there are children involved. This impact extends to your kids too. This reason is why it's so important to realize what you're dealing with and what you're up against.

Psychological Impact

Divorcing a narcissist can take a huge toll on your psychological well-being. Their constant manipulation, emotional games, and character attacks can lead to stress, anxiety, and even depression. You may experience a sense of helplessness, constantly questioning your reality due to the narcissist's deceitful tactics. The emotional manipulation can erode self-esteem and confidence, making it crucial for you to seek mental health support during and after the divorce. They may try to turn your children against you, tell them how bad and wrong you are, and how they are the victim. You can't react with toxicity; you need to be the mature parent in the situation. Let's face it, your child will need you. Don't you play the victim too, rather play the victor!

Financial Impact

Narcissists often employ tactics such as demanding excessive legal fees, hiding assets, and overwhelming the other party with paperwork. These maneuvers can drain your financial resources, making the divorce process emotionally challenging and financially burdensome. You may find it difficult to cover the escalating legal expenses, potentially leading to long-term financial repercussions. It becomes essential to have a strategic financial plan and a knowledgeable legal team to navigate these financial challenges.

Impact on the Children

Children often become unintended casualties in divorces involving narcissists. Tactics like using children as pawns, seeking full custody for manipulative reasons, and creating a hostile co-parenting environment can negatively affect the children's well-being. The constant turmoil and emotional manipulation can lead to behavioral issues, anxiety, and a strained relationship with both parents. It is crucial that you prioritize your children's needs, seek professional advice on co-parenting strategies, and, if necessary, involve the appropriate legal channels to protect your child(ren) from the negative impact of the narcissist's actions.

Your Defense Playbook

Divorcing from a narcissist can be a difficult and emotionally draining process, but there are defense strategies that can help counter the potential manipulative strategies a narcissist might employ during divorce proceedings. Here are some strategies based on the provided search results:

- **Witnesses:** Having witnesses who can testify to the narcissist's behavior can be helpful in court. Witnesses can include friends, family members, or professionals who have observed the narcissist's behavior.
- **Restraining orders:** If the narcissist is engaging in threatening or abusive behavior, a restraining order can be obtained to protect the victim.
- **Emotional resilience:** Building emotional resilience can help individuals withstand the emotional impact of divorcing a narcissist. Strategies for building emotional resilience include seeking therapeutic support, developing a support network, practicing mindfulness and self-care, and focusing on personal growth.
- **Financial audit:** Conducting a financial audit can help uncover any hidden assets or financial manipulation by the narcissist. This can be done by reviewing bank statements, tax returns, and other financial documents.
- **Forensic accountant:** A forensic accountant can be hired to investigate any financial manipulation by the narcissist and provide expert testimony in court.
- **Strategies for child custody:** These strategies include documenting involvement in the children's lives, arranging for neutral exchanges, developing a comprehensive parenting plan, and considering expert testimony.

By implementing these defense strategies, individuals can protect themselves and their interests when divorcing a narcissist. It is important to work with a lawyer who understands narcissism and has experience in handling high-conflict divorces.

Your Roadmap Through the Legal Maze

Let's face it, when it comes to a divorce challenge, the narcissist is in it to win it. You need to make sure you are as best prepared legally as you could possibly be. Ask yourself, what do you want? What can you control? What won't you tolerate? Base your strategy on the answers to these questions.

Getting Emotionally Ready

- Talk to friends, family, or a therapist for support.
- Take care of yourself and find ways to manage stress.
- Build a network of people who can help you through the divorce.

Handling Emotions

- Stay calm using the "gray rock" method to keep emotions in check.
- Use written communication like email to keep a record.
- Get a neutral third party involved for better communication.

Finding a Good Lawyer

- Pick a lawyer who is experienced and specializes in narcissistic behavior. We will discuss this in a bit more detail below.
- Share all the important information and evidence of manipulative actions with your lawyer.

Starting the Divorce Process

Here are three steps to follow when starting the divorce process:

1. Talk to your lawyer about the best plan.
2. Fill out the needed paperwork for the court.
3. Ensure your spouse gets the divorce papers.

Pros of starting first

- You take control of the divorce timeline.
- You set the pace for the process.

Cons of starting first

- You might provoke a strong reaction from your spouse.
- Their reaction could make the divorce more challenging.

Getting Finances Ready

Do your financial planning before you start initiating the divorce.

Financial preparations

- open a separate bank account
- choose a different bank
- make sure you have access to your accounts
- move funds to your new account

Listing assets

- write down all assets, like houses and cars
- figure out how much each one is worth

Monitor your credit report closely

- keep an eye on your credit report
- fix any mistakes or issues quickly

Money access

- be sure you have money for legal fees and other costs

Collecting and Showing Proof

Documenting all interactions with the narcissist can provide evidence to support your case in court.

Types of proof

- use written messages
- keep recordings of conversations
- get statements from witnesses

Organizing proof

- Sort your evidence by making a timeline and categories.
- Consider working with pros like private investigators or lawyers.

Striking a Fair Deal

When it comes to financial settlements, full disclosure, third-party valuation, and negotiation are crucial. It's important to work with a lawyer to develop a strategy that protects your financial interests.

- Be open about your income, assets, and debts to your spouse and their lawyer.
- Expert valuation: Bring in a pro appraiser to value assets, like property or valuables.
- Negotiating: Work with your lawyer to get a fair deal.

Splitting Assets

- Apply fair division strategies: List all assets. Think about each one's value and meaning. Try to agree on a fair split through talks or mediation.
- Legal choices: Ask your lawyer about the legal ways to divide assets.

Important Money Papers

- get your bank statements
- collect tax returns
- keep records of debts and investments

Parenting Plan

- You should make a detailed plan for parenting duties and kids' needs.
- You should talk to professionals like psychologists and counselors for extra support.
- Make sure you hold medical and school records for your children. Be patient and document everything. For example, if your ex-spouse missed taking your child to a doctor's appointment or did not show up to collect your child for the weekend, make notes of dates, times, and arrangements that were in place.

Support and Child Money

- You need to work with your lawyer to figure out fair alimony and child support.
- Remember to think about the financial needs of everyone involved.

Behaving in Court

- stay calm and collected
- speak clearly and to the point
- back up your words with evidence

When you follow these steps, you can navigate the legal system during your divorce, making the process smoother and more successful.

Fair Child Custody Moves

- keep records of your time with the kids
- show you can provide a stable and caring home
- get experts like psychologists to back your case
- write down your interactions with your kids
- gather proof of your involvement, like school reports
- arrange neutral kid exchanges to avoid conflicts

Choosing Your Champion

Narcissism is not widely understood by the general public, and it's not widely understood by lawyers. Narcissists have a sort of ripple effect, and they have an impact on multiple people in their lives. It's not just the spouse that's affected by the person's behavior. Of course, it affects their children too, which is a huge problem that can lead to narcissism passing down generations as a result of the behaviors that become learned. But they can also have problems at work or at home with their neighbors. They can have issues with their siblings, parents, cousins, and anyone they meet.

The step that's most important in initiating your divorce is to speak to a legal professional who is an expert in high-conflict cases, preferably divorces that involve narcissists. They will be able to educate you on the legal approaches you need to safeguard your interests.

When picking a lawyer to handle the case on your behalf, you need to keep a few things in mind:

- **Knowledge and experience:** Confirm that the lawyer has knowledge and expertise in managing cases with narcissistic personalities. Search for reviews from previous clients online and anonymously ask for advice on online support groups.
- **Expenses:** Familiarize yourself with the estimated fees to be charged by the specific lawyer. Discuss any concerns you may have in this regard with the lawyer.
- **Privacy:** Ensure that your meetings are private to safeguard any details shared that may be held against you when they fall into the wrong hands.

When picking a divorce lawyer for a case involving a narcissistic spouse, it's super important to check if they understand narcissism and can keep you safe. Find a bulldog—one who will choose their battles wisely. Here are some things to think about based on what I found:

Knowing Their Job

A lawyer who's dealt with divorces where one person is a narcissist can be like your shield and guide through all the legal stuff. They provide crucial support and know a lot about the law.

How They Look Out for You

A lawyer who's handled cases with narcissistic spouses can make sure your rights are protected. They can work on getting a fair deal for you and speak up for you in court. They're also good at coming up with plans to handle the tricky behavior of a narcissistic spouse, making sure you stay in control of what's happening.

Questions to Ask Lawyers

When you're talking to possible lawyers, think about asking them these questions to see if they're the right fit to help you:

- Have you worked with clients dealing with narcissistic spouses before?
- Can you give examples of cases like mine that you've successfully handled?
- What's your plan for dealing with the challenges that come with a narcissistic spouse during a divorce?
- What strategies do you think will help protect my interests and handle the narcissistic behavior during the divorce?

By really checking how much a lawyer understands about narcissism and if they can look out for you, you can make a smart choice when picking a lawyer for a divorce with a narcissistic spouse.

When Custody Battles Get Nasty

Carli went through a tough time when her wealthy ex, Nico, decided to take away their son simply to avoid paying child support. The injustice of it all made it incredibly difficult for Carli not to react and to resist firing back with anger and frustration. It was a real emotional challenge.

But you know what? The advice to not react was spot-on. Despite the court starting to label Carli as "crazy," echoing the tactics of an abuser, she resisted the temptation to respond. After a year of court battles, Carli learned that taking the bait only fueled Nico's satisfaction. It was like feeding a monster.

The lesson learned? Starve the monster. By not letting Nico's attempts to provoke a reaction succeed, Carli realized how empowering it was to stay composed. The more she stayed in control and didn't let emotions take over, the better she navigated challenging situation. Eventually, she won the legal battle to get her son to live with her with financial assistance from Nico and allow him regular visitation rights.

Going through a divorce and dealing with child custody battles can be incredibly tough. If you haven't been through it, you might not grasp how painful and devastating it is. And it's even worse when there are kids involved.

Many people worldwide are facing this challenge, and they often don't know how to handle a situation where a narcissist is making things difficult, especially in a high-conflict divorce. When you're up against a narcissist in court, they'll be telling lies about you and trying to charm everyone involved, including the court, lawyers, and experts. It's like they did when you first got together.

This is where having a specialized lawyer is crucial. They can level the playing field and even shift the momentum in your favor. Your lawyer will guide you on playing offense instead of just defense. It's about being proactive, staying calm, and not falling into the traps set by the narcissistic parent to make you look bad.

I get it—dealing with someone spreading lies about you, going from aggressive to playing the victim, can drive you crazy. That's why having a lawyer experienced in high-conflict divorces is so important, especially when kids are involved. They know how to navigate these tough situations and make sure your interests are protected.

Remember, this is not your or your child(ren)'s fault. The narcissist has deep-rooted issues that may be a result of neglect or other childhood trauma, or a generally low sense of self-worth, inflated by their act of being totally confident. You cannot change them. But you will need to make sure that they are not the main role model in your child's daily life. Do everything you can to fight for custody, but keep it cool, and don't allow their tactics to make you defensive. Don't allow their manipulation at all. Change your responses and manage them according to the legal behavior that you need to show. If you do something different than before, you will get a different reaction than before. So test this as a strategy and see what works best for you.

Making a mistake in how you handle legal matters can cost you custody of your child(ren). Follow the guidelines when it comes to sharing information willingly with the other party. Be aware of the laws in your specific country or state and know what information you should provide without waiting to be asked. Remember, the other party has to share information voluntarily as well.

When you receive discovery requests, you have an obligation to address them; don't just ignore them. Similarly, the other party is obligated to respond to your requests for information, documents, and admissions. Ignoring these requests might lead to automatically admitting statements, and it could result in extra attorney fees. So, it's crucial to stay on top of these legal responsibilities. If you are unsure about anything, always ask your lawyer.

Honesty is paramount when dealing with the court; never provide false information as it can severely impact your case. Lying undermines your credibility and can lead to serious consequences. Courts rely on accurate and truthful information to make fair decisions. If you're caught being dishonest, it can damage your reputation and credibility in the eyes of the court, potentially jeopardizing the outcome of your case. Always strive to present the facts truthfully, even if they may seem unfavorable. Being truthful not only upholds the integrity of the legal process but also enhances your chances of achieving a favorable resolution.

Maintaining respectful communication is another critical aspect. Avoid sending negative messages, making unpleasant phone calls, or sending disrespectful emails to the other parent, regardless of the circumstances. Being rude or disrespectful can be detrimental to your case, as the court may view you as the less cooperative partner and could potentially award custody to your ex-spouse. It's crucial to maintain a respectful and civil communication approach to uphold your standing in legal proceedings and contribute positively to the overall co-parenting dynamic.

Navigating custody battles requires a strategic and ethical approach. Following legal protocols, staying honest, and maintaining respectful communication are fundamental strategies to protect your interests and contribute to a favorable outcome.

INTERACTIVE ELEMENT: BREAKOUT BOX

Key point: preparation is power.

Navigating the complexities of divorcing a narcissist requires strategic preparation. Here's your guide to empowerment:

- **Legal strategy:** Determine your approach early on. Recognize the distinct challenges involved in divorcing a narcissist, such as psychological warfare and uncooperative behaviors.
- **Recognize manipulative tactics:** Understand the tactics narcissists may use during legal proceedings, from delaying tactics to character assassination. Forewarned is forearmed; knowledge is your shield.
- **Roadmap to success:** Follow a roadmap that covers emotional preparation, securing effective legal counsel, and practical steps for financial preparations. Each step is a move toward a smoother process.
- **Defensive playbook:** Arm yourself with defense strategies. Make a paper trail for everything, build your emotional resilience, and protect your finances. Your playbook ensures you're ready for any move.
- **Choosing your champion:** Selecting the right attorney is crucial. Ask questions about their experience, understand their role in protecting you, and review their past cases. Your attorney is your champion.

Remember: Your preparation becomes your strongest defense and empowers you to face the challenges ahead.

In this chapter, we delved into the legal battlefield of divorcing a narcissist, using Carlos and Nina's story as a backdrop. The chapter emphasized the importance of preparation, offering you a comprehensive guide to navigating the complexities of divorce. From legal strategies to defensive playbooks, the key takeaway is clear: preparation is power.

————

As we move forward, the narrative transitions to a topic of utmost importance: the well-being of the children involved. Chapter 6, "Keeping the Kids' Best Interests at Heart," explores the unique challenges parents face when divorcing a narcissist. We'll navigate the intricacies of child custody, parenting plans, and support strategies, ensuring that the children emerge from the process with their best interests at the forefront. Join us as we navigate the emotional landscape of co-parenting amid the complexities of divorcing a narcissist.

Before we continue, I want to acknowledge that not everyone navigating a divorce from a narcissist has children. I see you, and your experience is just as valid and important. While some chapters may specifically address parenting aspects, the principles and support shared can be universally applied. Feel free to skip ahead or focus on the chapters that resonate most with your unique situation. This book is for everyone seeking strength, healing, and a brighter tomorrow, regardless of the family structure you may be navigating. Your journey matters, and the aim of this book is to support you every step of the way.

6. Keeping the Kids' Best Interests at Heart

Children need models rather than critics.

— Joseph Joubert

Macy faces challenges co-parenting with George, who consistently undermines her authority. George uses their children as pawns in his emotional games. He tries to turn the kids against Macy by sharing negative stories about her. George intentionally doesn't enforce any rules at his house, allowing late bedtimes, junk food, and no homework, to be the "fun" parent.

Macy wrestles with an internal conflict, torn between wanting her children to have a father figure and protecting them from George's manipulative tendencies. She notices a change in her children's behavior and attitude toward her after they spend time with George. She seeks counseling, both for herself and for her children, to navigate the complex dynamics.

The therapist provides Macy with strategies to rebuild her bond with her children and counteract George's influence. Macy starts setting aside time for one-on-one conversations with each child, creating a safe space for them to express their feelings.

She listens to their concerns without judgment and validates their feelings. Macy explains her reasons for certain rules, emphasizing that they stem from love and concern for their well-being.

Over time, with consistent communication, the children begin to understand and trust Macy's intentions. As the kids grow up and become more discerning, they start to see through George's tactics.

They begin to appreciate the stability, structure, and genuine care Macy provides, contrasting it with the chaos and manipulation they experience with George.

Co-parenting with a narcissist? No, let's call it counter-parenting because they need to be in control of everything, including the children. Co-parenting is when both parents are on board to reach mutual ground for their child's best interest. Whereas narcissistic parents only seek their own gain and break the rules as they like. In this chapter, we explore parallel parenting with a narcissist. When you apply parallel parenting, you make sure to be physically and emotionally unattached from the narcissist during the parenting process. As we continue, you will gain strategies for making the best out of your situation.

STEP 6—(O)UTLINE PARALLEL PARENTING PLANS

So, what exactly is parallel parenting, as opposed to "shared" or co-parenting? Co-parenting suggests that separated parents do things collaboratively for the sake of their mutual child. But in the concept of parallel parenting, the parents avoid being present together at the same functions, appointments, or events, also for the best interest of their child. In parallel parenting agreements, communication mainly occurs via electronic mail, text messages, or mobile co-parenting applications (Communication in a Parallel Parenting Arrangement, n.d.).

Parenting with a narcissist may be highly difficult, and the issues experienced by parents are similar. Narcissistic parents frequently push limits and breach commitments to satisfy their wants above all others. They could find it difficult to follow through on commitments, be unaccommodating, and include the kids in arguments between both parents. Additionally, they may use manipulation, criticize parenting, and exhibit poor boundaries, making co-parenting a complete nightmare (Brown, 2023).

The impact of such dynamics on children can be severe, leading to emotional trauma and long-term consequences. Understanding and validating these experiences is crucial, and in this chapter, we will explore strategies for navigating parenting with a narcissist while prioritizing the well-being of both your child and yourself.

You're Not Just Imagining It

For young children to have effective intellectual growth, they only require a single primary caregiver who is consistently present, receptive, and approachable (Akin, 2023). This is wonderful news if you don't see a future for shared parenting with your ex-spouse!

Parenting together with a narcissist is challenging mostly because of post-breakup mistreatment. Even when the relationship ends, a narcissistic person will continue to feel destined to hold onto their position of control and dominance. Shared parenting with a self-absorbed parent can have serious repercussions for you and your young ones if done improperly.

Co-parenting with a narcissist can be emotionally exhausting and may turn into a big fight over custody. This situation can be really tough for single parents after a divorce. The narcissistic parent is mostly focused on themselves and might use the kids to get what they want. This can mess up how parents work together, causing a lot of problems like manipulation, criticism, and bad boundaries.

Narcissists want to control everything, even parenting. They might see their kids as just extensions of themselves, caring more about what they want than being responsible parents. Trying to co-parent with a narcissist isn't a good idea. It's better to consider parallel parenting, which means both parents are more separate but still involved in the kids' lives. This approach helps cut down on conflicts and ensures everyone, including the kids, stays okay (Hill, n.d.).

Parallel parenting involves disengaging from the other parent as much as possible, communicating only when necessary, and creating a detailed parenting plan to establish firm boundaries and minimize opportunities for manipulation and power plays.

Narcissistic parents see their job as moms and dads in a different way compared to regular parents. They're more about getting their kids to keep making them feel good about themselves. These parents expect their kids to make them feel important, no matter how the kids act. It's like everything has to be about them, even when their kids are involved. They use their kids' successes to make themselves look good and feel better about themselves.

Kids of narcissistic parents often end up taking on specific roles, like being the favorite child, the one blamed for everything, the unnoticed one, the truth-teller, or the one who always has to take care of everything (Thomas, 2023). These roles show how everyone in the family acts and what's expected of them. Narcissistic parents treat their kids like they're just parts of themselves, caring more about what they want than being good parents. They find it hard to think about others and often seem uninterested in what their kids need or feel.

Growing up with a narcissistic parent can really mess with a kid's mental health, causing emotional pain and long-term problems. It could lead your child to have lower self-esteem and drive them to set overly ambitious goals. But knowing more about personality disorders, being able to tell when someone is just talking and not doing anything, and being aware of yourself can help you figure out and handle problems in your friendships, relationships, and work. If things are tough, talking to a professional can give you a safe space to sort out your feelings, work on your self-esteem, and learn good ways to deal with stuff.

Narcissistic parents can be possessive and supercritical, and they can like to control their kids. They worry that their children might become independent, so they do things to stop it, like embarrassing or making them feel ashamed. They often use their children to get what they want and can't handle being criticized. Sometimes, they trick their kids and act like they're the ones being treated badly.

Parallel Parenting Versus Co-Parenting

Parallel parenting is a co-parenting approach designed for separated couples dealing with high-conflict situations. The narcissistic parent worries that their children might become independent, so they do things to stop it, like embarrassing or making them feel ashamed. The overarching goal of limited communication in parallel parenting is to minimize conflict and provide children with a predictable and less stressful environment.

Here are some examples of limited communication in parallel parenting:

- **Remote communication:** Instead of in-person discussions, parents communicate through emails, texts, or online messaging services. For example, discussing school events, medical appointments, or logistical details through email can maintain a structured and documented exchange.
- **Businesslike communication:** Communication is kept straightforward, focusing on the children's needs and avoiding emotional topics. An example is a brief text exchange about pick-up and drop-off times without delving into personal matters.
- **Journaling:** Some parents keep a journal to record essential details about their child's behavior, illnesses, or significant events. For instance, noting down a child's reaction to a particular situation or keeping track of medical appointments for future reference.
- **Scheduling events:** Parents divide events and activities between them, taking turns to attend and avoiding overlapping schedules. For example, one parent may attend a school play while the other takes the child to a sports event on a different date, ensuring both parents remain involved without direct interaction.
- **Limited contact:** Parents may refrain from communicating directly or restrict communication with legal representatives. An example could be utilizing legal channels to discuss and resolve issues related to child custody without direct communication between the parents.
- **Neutral communication:** Communication remains neutral, with each parent establishing their own rules and making independent parenting decisions. An example is

discussing school-related decisions, such as homework routines, in a straightforward and non-confrontational manner.

However, it's crucial to note that while this approach can empower parents with a sense of independence, it may unintentionally create a sense of disconnection for the child if negative messages about the other parent are conveyed. These examples illustrate practical applications of limited communication strategies in the parallel parenting model, emphasizing the focus on the well-being of the children involved.

Children in the Crossfire

Imagine dealing with an ex who's all about themselves and what they want. Parenting with a narcissistic ex can be a real headache. They might use the kids as pawns, turning parenting into a power game that makes things difficult for everyone, especially the children.

Think about a situation where your ex always needs to be the star, gets super upset over any criticism, and loves to play the victim. This kind of behavior can mess with your kids, making it tough for them to trust, say what they need, or form healthy relationships.

It's like a never-ending emotional rollercoaster, with your ex pulling the strings and the kids getting stuck in different roles, like being the favorite or the one blamed for everything. This doesn't just mess with them now; it can have long-lasting effects as they grow up.

Trying to figure out this new parenting situation is like walking on a tightrope. Getting professional help is crucial in dealing with the challenges and making sure your kids are okay. It's a bumpy road, but with the right support, things can get better for both you and the kids.

Children raised by narcissistic parents frequently ignore their own needs in an effort to stay out of trouble or avoid their parent's rage, resulting in them feeling as though no one is interested in them. With fluctuating moods and emotional tricks abound in their household, they risk becoming excessively independent or overly dependent on others.

These children struggle as they become older to establish healthy relationships, set limits, and express their needs and feelings. As they get older, these issues don't simply go away; they persist, which is why therapy and self-awareness are essential for recovery and fostering stronger relationships.

Children who have narcissistic parents may also have trouble building safe connections, trusting others, and avoiding becoming narcissistic themselves. All of this may have a profound effect, leading to issues such as difficulty establishing boundaries, insecurities, a lack of self-worth, and even managing depression and feelings of anxiousness. Sometimes, these children are so accustomed to their parents' conduct that they fail to see that it is abnormal, only realizing the harm when they are adults if they ever come to self-realization.

You need to maintain the "no contact" rule, even when you are parallel parenting. Don't allow them around you in your presence for the sake of the children. This is your enemy and will not do your children any good if you are around them. Protect yourself, and protect your children. Communicate with them only by email or record all your phone conversations.

To simplify things, you can also consider using a custody arrangement app (check what's allowed by the court first, though). This will ensure that you have no other contact with your ex, and also leave a paper trail of all your interactions and arrangements. Investigate apps like Talking Parents, WeParent, Our Family Wizard, Cozi, Google Calendar, App Close, Custody Connection, and 2 Houses.

Growing up with narcissistic parents can create a lot of challenges for kids, affecting how they feel about themselves and how they navigate relationships. Here's a breakdown:

- **Confusion:** Imagine not knowing what to expect from your parent because their behavior is all over the place. Kids of narcissistic parents often feel confused due to inconsistent actions and emotional manipulation. It's like dealing with different versions of the same person.
- **Divided commitment:** There's a struggle for these children in terms of loyalty. They often feel responsible for meeting their parent's needs and are expected to serve them. This dynamic can make it hard for them to form healthy boundaries and connect emotionally with others.
- **Guilt:** These kids may carry a heavy load of guilt, shame, and fear. They're conditioned to believe they're not "good enough" through constant emotional and psychological abuse. This can make them feel uneasy about succeeding or being in the spotlight.

Now, let's discuss the lasting impacts:

- **Emotional turmoil:** Dealing with a narcissistic parent is emotionally draining. It can lead to anxiety, depression, self-doubt, and problems managing emotions. So, these kids often feel uneasy and unsure about their feelings.
- **Impaired emotional development:** To cope, some children suppress their own feelings to meet their parent's needs. Unfortunately, this can affect their emotional

growth, making it challenging to form healthy relationships later in life.

- **Low self-esteem:** Constant criticism and manipulation can weaken a child's confidence. They end up having low self-worth and struggle to see themselves positively.

In a nutshell, kids of narcissistic parents often deal with confusion, guilt, and loyalty issues, which stick with them, affecting their self-esteem and emotional well-being. This, in turn, can make it challenging for them to have healthy relationships and manage their emotions.

Shielding Kids From Narcissistic Fallout

In the event of a marriage ending in divorce or the separation of single parents, it is expected that the two will collaborate in a co-parenting agreement to lessen the effects of the separation on their children. Many Family Court experts believe that parents must figure out how to co-parent. This is apparent in their directives to the court, despite the fact that there is enough proof that these parents are at war with one another and that their continual appearance in court adds to this belief. Trying to "command" antagonistic parents to co-parent really exacerbates the issue.

Unfortunately, there isn't a way to steer clear of this if both parties don't cooperate. When dealing with a parent with a big ego and who tends to be self-centered, it's important to focus on protecting your child from the emotional impact. Here are some simple ways to help your child (Durvasula, 2021; Farzad, n.d.):

- **Be the chill parent:** Make sure the kids feel calm and secure, especially during a divorce with a self-centered parent.

- **Stick to a routine:** Keep things consistent and predictable to give the kids stability.
- **Don't fall into drama:** Avoid reacting emotionally to the self-centered parent's attempts to make you look like the bad guy.
- **Avoid criticizing the narcissistic parent:** Do not speak poorly of the narcissistic parent in front of the child, as it can confuse them and damage their relationship with the parent. Rather use general statements when talking about acceptable or unacceptable adult behavior.
- **Don't gaslight your child:** Protect kids from being manipulated and lied to by a self-centered parent. Make sure they have a safe and calm place to go after spending time with that parent, and create a peaceful home environment for them.
- **Keep your distance:** Try to have as little contact as possible and use the tools you have to initiate arrangements regarding your child's care.
- **Support and avoid blaming:** Validate the kids' feelings and avoid talking badly about the self-centered parent in front of them.
- **Stop abuse and teach coping skills:** Take action if the child is being mistreated and teach them how to manage their emotions.
- **Create a caring home space:** Make sure the home is a supportive and understanding place for the kids, especially if they live away from the self-centered parent.
- **Get professional support:** Encourage the kids to see a counselor or therapist to deal with any emotional issues caused by the self-centered parent.

- **Keep yourself grounded and firm**: Avoid emotional reactions that the narcissistic parent may use to paint you as the bad parent. Stay calm and consistent to provide stability for the children.
- **Prevent abuse from the other parent:** Shield the child from emotional abuse, gaslighting, and lies by the narcissistic parent. Provide a safe and peaceful home environment for the child, and seek professional help to address any emotional issues.
- **Teach self-regulation and self-soothing:** Help the child develop self-regulation and self-soothing techniques to cope with the stress and emotional manipulation caused by the narcissistic parent.
- **Keep track of wrongdoing and carry out court orders:** Remember that document keeping? Add a page for any wrongdoing on the part of the narcissistic parent and uphold any court orders to protect your child's welfare and safety.

When you implement these strategies, you can help protect your child from the negative effects of having a narcissistic parent and support them in coping with the situation.

When parallel parenting fails, what should you do? How do you find resilience during this disruptive and difficult stage in your life? Resilience means you recover quickly from difficult situations or keep standing when challenged. When conflict is high, and you need to be on defense the entire time, it drains you emotionally and physically. This is when you need to be resilient, ground yourself, recover to function in your new normal, and make the correct decisions.

First, being aware that you are a bit shaken and admitting it is an important step in acknowledging what you're experiencing. Then, you need to identify something constructive to focus on; you will know the rest is only noise, and you will keep your focus point without wavering. You need to constantly remind yourself not to get distracted from your main purpose.

Making It Work

You are prioritizing your children's needs over yours when you act in their best interests. A narcissist prioritizes their own desires. There are many things one can do to set limitations, safeguard yourself, and safeguard your kids even when you cannot change the other person's behavior or make them conscious of their issue.

Create a Parenting Strategy

Creating a parenting strategy might involve more than just deciding on child custody; it also consists of defining the guidelines and principles you want your kid to be brought up with.

The right attorney will understand your need for a direct and detailed parenting plan. The ideal time to establish one is during the divorce process when you have a family law expert assisting you with some of the concerns that go into establishing one.

If your divorce landed you with little more than a rough draft of a custody plan, you can still work with a parenting consultant to create a workable plan.

Establish Interaction Guidelines

You may remain factual with your former partner by establishing clear communication limits. Since narcissists frequently take pleasure in being able to elicit a response from you, try to keep your feelings to yourself. Additionally, they can attempt to use those replies against you by painting you as a "harmful person." Having email and text conversations instead of phone calls can help with this.

Set Clear Rules for Co-Parenting

During a divorce, it's crucial to stick to the plan you and your ex agreed upon. One simple way to do this is by acknowledging and appreciating when your ex follows the plan. Since narcissistic individuals often seek approval, you might encourage them to keep up their positive behavior by praising their efforts. If this doesn't work, legal intervention may be necessary. If the reinforcement approach doesn't yield results, the next step could involve legal action. The key is to present it as a potential consequence before taking any legal steps. Judges typically believe it's in the best interest of the child to maintain regular contact with both parents, even though they may reconsider the terms of the divorce if one parent has behaved poorly. Ensuring everyone follows the agreed-upon rules helps create a more stable environment for the child.

Parent Empathizing: Refrain From Making Fun of Your Ex

If you talk poorly about your former partner to your kids, they could feel bad about themselves for wanting to hang out with their other parent. This behavior may stress the bond between you and the other parent or between your child and the other parent. Since parents teach their children how to behave, modeling appropriate behavior in all relationships will have a beneficial effect on them. Their perception of what is appropriate in their personal relationships may be influenced if they witness you acting or speaking harshly toward the other parent.

Take Your Child Out of the Center

Some details of the separation might be harmful for your child to know; therefore, they are not required to understand every detail. It is not necessary to know the particular reasons for the divorce or the way it transpired, even for teens who may be more cognizant of what went down. They don't have to know everything, but there must be a balance so they don't end up as pawns in the end. Your child shouldn't be forced to cope with the stress of handling conflicts between them and their other parent.

Make the Most of Therapy

Parenting together with a narcissistic ex will be easier if you have a supportive group or a competent therapist you can turn to. You need somebody to keep you balanced since narcissists may make you feel insane and even actively attempt to do so. Counseling is a terrific choice for anybody looking to improve their coping mechanisms in this scenario or for any other issue. In addition, you might have a better understanding of your circumstances by consulting with a qualified practitioner. After a separation or divorce, you require the same level of assistance that you did throughout the divorce process.

Take Charge of What You Can Manage

You have the power to regulate your feelings and your actions. Since you can't control your ex's actions, begin the process of transformation within. Deny narcissists their desires because they thrive on feelings and conflict. Seek a constructive way to release your anger, like exercising or constructive redirection.

Legal Factors to Take Into Account

It's vital that you know your legal rights. Understanding a comprehensive custody arrangement may be somewhat challenging, therefore it could be beneficial to have a lawyer explain your options in detail. If you satisfy the qualifications, these custody arrangements can be changed, but any changes are likely to be challenged, particularly if you're dealing with a narcissist. Having a *guardian ad litem* assigned would probably work to your advantage if you end up in court since they will look out for your child's best interests.

Get Ready

Learn what works and what doesn't when you're dealing with a co-parent. Generally speaking, you and the other parties are better off reducing touch to a minimum and interacting briefly.

Factors to Consider When You Decide on Pursuing Full Custody

When deciding whether to pursue full custody, consider these factors (Wolf, 2020):

- **Child's well-being:** The welfare of the child in question is the court's top priority, and it is crucial to consider what is in the child's greatest interest. The court looks at how the kids will be impacted if they keep things as they are with the current custody plan or if they change it. They want to figure out what's best for the children and how any changes might affect them.
- **Learning, psychological, and bodily needs:** The court takes into account the needs of the kid in terms of education, emotional support, and physical well-being, as well as any potential effects of the shift in circumstances. When deciding which parent should take care of the kids, the court looks at how well each parent can meet their basic needs like food and shelter, make sure they're emotionally okay, and provide medical care when needed.

- **Personal character witnesses:** They also listen to what people who know each parent will have to say about their character.
- **Child's desires and feelings:** Given the child's age and comprehension level, the court considers the child's wishes and feelings.
- **Their personal history:** The gender, age, and any unique needs of the kid are considered by the court.
- **Parental fitness:** A parent may be deemed unsuitable if they exhibit a lack of interest in their kid or are dealing with difficulties such as substance abuse or mental health concerns.

There will be many documents and forms to complete to apply for full custody. Work with your lawyer when considering full custody, as custody battles can be complex and contentious. They can help you navigate the process and make well-thought-out choices based on the situation. Should the time come to go to court, make sure that you show up and that you are dressed neatly (Washington, 2022).

BREAKOUT BOX: YOUR CHILD'S WELLBEING COMES FIRST

Even though Macy faced challenges co-parenting with George, she bravely tried out strategies to rebuild her bond with her children and counteract his influence. By doing so, she created a safe space for her children to express their feelings.

Let's recap on a few important points mentioned in this chapter:

- **Pick your battles carefully:** Steer clear of pointless confrontations and pick your battles carefully. Put your attention on what matters most and set aside little arguments.
- **Maintain your space and prevent disagreement:** Try your best to avoid conflict and maintain a respectful distance from your narcissistic ex-partner. By doing so, you can lessen stress and safeguard your mental health.
- **Keep interaction brief, straightforward, and businesslike:** To prevent miscommunication and lessen tension, communicate with your ex-partner in a brief, businesslike way.
- **Emergency measures:** To keep your kids safe in an emergency, get legal counsel and secure emergency orders.

In this chapter, we delved into the complexities of co-parenting with a narcissist, offering readers valuable strategies to navigate such challenging situations. The focus was on upholding agreed-upon frameworks during a divorce and fostering a stable environment for the children involved.

————

Now, as we transition into the next chapter, titled "A Future Where You're Truly Free," we'll explore the journey beyond the immediate challenges of co-parenting with a narcissist. Building upon the strategies discussed earlier, we'll delve into ways to reclaim personal freedom and move toward a future where individuals can thrive independently despite the lingering impact of a challenging co-parenting dynamic.

7. A Future Where You're Truly Free

Moving forward is the only way to survive.

— Tahereh Mafi

In her new place, Aisha sat surrounded by stuff she chose, making her apartment feel like her own. It wasn't just about finding a new spot; it was like she found herself again after dealing with Roger's way of doing things for so long.

See, Aisha and Roger used to be a team, but Roger took over—deciding what they'd have and how it'd look. Aisha went along to keep the peace, but it made her feel like she wasn't really herself. Roger didn't just disagree with her choices; he made her doubt who she was and what she wanted.

But then, things changed. Aisha moved into a new home, and the empty rooms felt a bit scary but also cool. It was a chance for her to be herself again. So, she started with little things, like picking out her own coffee mug, choosing curtains she liked, and getting a plant she thought was cool. They were small choices, but they meant a lot to her.

As she sat in her living room one evening, surrounded by the things she picked out, Aisha felt proud. It wasn't just about how nice her place looked; it was like she found herself again through the process. Decorating her place became a way for her to trust herself and start a journey to being true to who she really is.

Welcome to a chapter that unfolds the pages of life after divorce from a narcissist. It's a chapter that echoes the stories of those who've weathered the storm, like Aisha, and came out on the other side with newfound strength and resilience.

As we navigate through these pages, we dive into the intricacies of rebuilding when the echoes of a narcissistic relationship still linger. The focus is on moving forward, not just geographically (if possible) but also emotionally and mentally, reclaiming what was lost, and discovering the courage to be true to yourself.

Just like Aisha, many have faced the challenge of redefining life after the divorce papers are signed. It's about finding yourself, becoming more independent, and regaining confidence in your decisions. This chapter is a guide, offering practical insights and empowering narratives to help you move beyond the shadows of a narcissistic past.

Let's turn the page together and explore the transformative journey that follows the end of a narcissistic marriage. Let's find the tools and inspiration needed to rebuild, rediscover, and move forward into a life that is authentically yours.

STEP 7—(M)OVE FORWARD

In the tumultuous aftermath of a narcissistic marriage and divorce, your journey toward healing begins with a profound surrender—the relinquishment of your ego that masked the painful truths. This pivotal moment signifies a departure from self-deception and an embrace of unfiltered honesty. The inner peace that ensues, previously elusive, now becomes a beacon guiding your way forward.

To deny reality and live in a realm of avoidance is to choose stagnation over growth and, ultimately, death over life. The acknowledgment that one can no longer deceive oneself initiates a perspective-changing process marked by the courage to confront suppressed emotions, especially the formidable forces of anger and fear. The path to enlightenment demands an unwavering commitment to self-truth—an acknowledgment that resonates in the light of consciousness.

This journey is not one to be traversed alone, for the interconnected nature of humanity beckons for communal support. The narrative underscores the imperative to seek assistance in the pursuit of evolution, dispelling the misconception that isolation is a refuge. The call to connect with trusted allies echoes the understanding that thriving in solitude is an impossibility for humans.

Discard your armor of self-imposed solitude and lean on the strength derived from your collective human experience.

Based on my own experience, the advice is to break down the emotional walls we've built because of past pain. It encourages recognizing our natural ability to love and show kindness. This realization is like discovering a special gift we all have—the ability to both give and receive love.

I would like to stress the importance of tapping into the positive energy within ourselves. It's like having the power to brighten our own lives every day, just like the sun rises. Living genuinely, being honest with ourselves, and understanding what we can and cannot control is the key to a conscious and happy life. We can make this decision every day when we wake up.

As the chapter unfolds, we explore exactly how to move forward after a stormy divorce from a narcissistic partner. We focus on being strong, learning more about ourselves, and making the choice to find happiness despite a difficult past.

It's Okay to Not Be Okay

The end of a marriage or a relationship is accompanied by a wide range of emotions, which are often intensified after leaving a relationship with a narcissist. You may feel angry, sad, relieved, confused, guilty, or doubtful. These feelings are totally normal. You are going through a very difficult time, and you need to be kind to yourself to survive.

It's totally fine if you're feeling not okay right now. Going through a divorce is tough, even if things are amicable. It's a normal part of the process to grieve and work through the losses that come with it. Give yourself the permission to feel and handle these emotions in your own time. Here are some practical tips to help you navigate this difficult period:

- **Be kind to yourself:** Let yourself go through the emotions, even if they're hard or unexpected.
- **Accept your difficult, confusing feelings:** It's okay to feel a mix of emotions like sadness, relief, loneliness, anger, and grief.

- **Release past love:** Let it go. Recognize the losses and deal with the emotions tied to the end of your marriage.
- **Ask for help:** Talk to people you trust or a therapist for understanding and some guidance.
- **Take care of yourself:** Do things that bring you joy and help you relax, like exercising, reading, or spending time outdoors.
- **Be patient with yourself:** Grieving takes time, and your feelings might change from day to day or week to week.

Remember, your grief is valid, and you're not alone. Be gentle with yourself, and give yourself the time and space you need to get through this time in your life.

Discover Who You Are Without Them

Navigating a divorce from a narcissist can be a draining journey, leaving you feeling lost and disconnected from who you are. Yet, there's a chance to embark on a path of self-discovery and rediscover your authentic identity. Here are some suggestions to help you find yourself again:

- **Take a necessary break:** Allow yourself time to adapt to the end of the relationship and the absence of your partner. Take a step back from the relationship and focus on your own well-being.
- **Re-establish with your inner child:** Recall the activities you enjoyed before the relationship and reconnect with your inner child. Participate in activities that foster happiness and relaxation.
- **Develop new habits:** Initiate a variety of new experiences. Whether it's taking a road trip, trying skydiving, or even

relocating to another country, open yourself up to new possibilities.

- **Reflect on your past:** Ponder past experiences to make sense of them. This reflection can aid in understanding how the narcissistic relationship may have impacted your sense of self.
- **Remain in the moment:** Concentrate on the current moment without dwelling on the past or worrying about the future. Mindfulness practices like meditation or yoga can assist in staying present.
- **Enjoy recreational activities:** Participate in activities that bring happiness, fun, and rest, such as hobbies, spending time with friends, or trying new things.
- **Acknowledge your personal power:** Remind yourself that you possess the power to shape the life you desire. Concentrate on your strengths and your aspirations in life.

Your journey to understanding yourself takes time and patience. Be gentle with yourself and grant yourself the space needed to genuinely reconnect.

Who Were You Before the Relationship?

Reflecting on who you were before is an essential step in understanding the impact the relationship had on your identity. Think about the person you once were, the values you held, and the activities that brought you joy before the relationship began. Write it down.

Consider what has changed since then. Did you notice any major changes in your beliefs, preferences, or behaviors? Perhaps the relationship influenced the way you chose your priorities or how you saw yourself when looking in the mirror? Identifying these changes is crucial for reclaiming aspects of your authentic self.

Recognize what remains of your core self. Write it down, too. Despite the challenges faced in the relationship, certain fundamental aspects of your identity may still be present. These could be your values, passions, or innate characteristics that withstand the trials you've experienced.

This introspection helps you separate the external influences from your intrinsic self. It's a way to start finding and getting back in touch with the most important parts of who you are. Understanding both the changes and the enduring elements of your identity sets the foundation for personal growth and the journey toward a more authentic self.

I want to make this point super clear—you don't need to aim to be the same person you were before dealing with the narcissist. That's not the goal here, and it's totally okay. What you've been through has changed you, and that's okay too. Instead of trying to go back, focus on how you've grown.

Think of it this way: you're not going in reverse; you're progressing ahead with all the strength and wisdom you've acquired. It's about embracing the lessons, understanding the changes, and using them to become an even more kick-ass version of yourself. So don't stress about going back—you're on a journey of growth, and everyone who loves you is cheering you on every step of the way!

It's impossible to go back to exactly how you were before your relationship. It damaged you, and no matter how much effort you put into undoing it, some changes are just there. It's not about erasing the past but finding a new and improved version of yourself. You've been through some stuff, and that has shaped you. Embracing that change and using it to figure out who you want to be now is where your real power lies. You can totally rethink, adjust, and find yourself. With who you are now and what you want in your life. So take your time, explore, and let yourself evolve. You've got this!

Enduring such a difficult relationship can really make you feel lost. It's essential to take some time to figure out what you really want in life. Here are some questions to help you with that (Brown, n.d):

- **Which hobbies did I have before the relationship?** Take a moment to think about the things you enjoyed doing and who you were at that time.
- **At that point, what was I searching for in life?** Think about what you wanted in life before this relationship. Your answer can help you understand what you might want now.
- **What has this relationship taught me about me?** Consider what you've learned about yourself during this relationship. Understanding how this experience affected how you see yourself is important.
- **What do I currently desire from my relationships with other people and life?** Think about what you want for your life and relationships now. This thinking can help you set goals and work toward the kind of life you want.
- **What matters to me right now?** Take a moment to think about what matters to you right now. This self-awareness can help you focus on what's really important.

Rediscovering yourself takes a while. I'm reminding you again—be kind to yourself. If you need help, talk to friends, family, or your therapist. I also want to encourage you to do things that fulfill you and help you relax and recharge your mind and body. Rediscovering yourself is not just possible, it's really important Taking the time to do it is like giving yourself superpowers to rescue your future!

Reclaiming Your Voice

If you're struggling to find the right words to communicate your story to others, whether it's friends, family, lawyers, or therapists, don't worry—it's more common than you think. Making your story clear and creating a connection is not always easy, especially when you've faced trauma or have memories that may steer you away from your original narrative.

One thing that can make it challenging is when others find it hard to understand, they might tune you out. To avoid this, try taking some deep breaths to make sure you don't rush through your words. It's crucial to share your story with those who can provide support during this process, but that doesn't mean you have to be ready to tell everyone just yet.

Before opening up to more people, make sure you're emotionally strong enough to handle it. It's okay to take your time and choose who you feel comfortable sharing your story with. The goal is to help others understand you better and foster a connection, and taking care of yourself along the way is just as important.

When No One Comes to Rescue You—Save Yourself

You are enough and you deserve a great life. Unfortunately, in this traumatic time of our lives, we want a hero in some form to come and rescue us and make everything better. There may not be such a hero, but the great news is that there is still hope for you to rise from the ashes and reclaim and improve your life.

We are always seeking for external validation. It may stem from our childhood, where we wanted our parents or teachers to tell us that we were on the right path. We keep on seeking the green light for self-worth throughout our lives, and even in intimate relationships.

When you are divorced, you find yourself alone and responsible for so many things. You suddenly wish you were a child again, carefree, or that you have someone to come and rescue you. You may wish you had people in your life to relieve the excess weight on your shoulders.

When you have children it can be a difficult time: There are decisions to make about school, studies, finances, and the list goes on. It's a lot of responsibility to take. But you need to know that as hard as it is when you're narcissist ex decides not to be involved or you are parallel parenting, the reality is that you have all the responsibility to manage, and you need to push through and keep doing it.

That being said, you are only human, and you don't have to be so hard on yourself. Also, just as responsible as you are for your children, finances, and other responsibilities, you are responsible for yourself and your wellness. So, you need to make time for yourself to rest, have a break, and treat yourself occasionally. Take a day off, and do something you enjoy.

Don't expect that someone will come and save you. Be your own greatest hero. Stay strong. And keep the right people in your life who will support you, even though they can't solve all the issues you are facing.

Charting the Course

Planning for life after divorce is a pivotal step toward moving forward and creating opportunities for personal growth. The following comprehensive tips can guide you in charting the course for your life after divorce:

- **Establish your objectives:** Make sure to spend time setting objectives for the near future as well as for the long term. This process will help you remain focused and work toward the life you envision.
- **Be SMART:** Guarantee that goals are Specific, Measurable, Achievable, Relevant, and Time-bound (Leonard & Watts, 2022). This approach ensures the creation of clear and attainable objectives for your future.
- **Reflect on your needs and aspirations:** Consider what you desire for your future, including the well-being of your children, if applicable. This reflection is instrumental in prioritizing values and concentrating on what matters most.
- **Create a plan:** Create a comprehensive strategy for achieving your goals, taking gradual steps toward the life you envision.
- **Take a much-needed break:** Allow yourself the necessary time to adapt to changes and the absence of your partner. Taking a break and focusing on self-care is crucial for emotional well-being.
- **Re-establish a self-connection:** Find the things that make you happy and relaxed. Do things that make you feel good and bring you joy.
- **Stay focused on the here and now:** Without thinking too much about the past or stressing about what's to come, stay focused on now. Mindfulness activities such as meditation or yoga can help you stay centered.
- **Seek support:** Reach out to friends, family, or a therapist for guidance and understanding during this challenging time. Building a support system is crucial for navigating the complexities of life after divorce.

Life after divorce involves a process of adjustment and acceptance, offering opportunities for personal growth and new beginnings. Be kind to yourself, allow the space you need, and embrace the chance to chart a course for your life after divorce.

Rebuilding Your Finances After Divorce

Rebuilding your finances after a divorce might seem impossible, but it is possible if you use the appropriate techniques (The Harris Law Firm, 2023):

- **Starting with financial clarity:** The initial step in repairing money after splitting up is gaining transparency about your finances. Gaining control over your earnings, outlays, possessions, and debts is necessary for this step. You need to know exactly how much income is being brought in, where it's going, and how much of it you actually have available.
- **Creating a fresh financial plan:** A key element of financial healing is creating an entirely new strategy that takes your post-divorce finances into account. Your new plan should help you live within what you can afford by taking into alterations in income and spending. If your out-of-pocket costs are more than the money you make, find ways to simplify and reduce your expenses.
- **Restoring credibility:** Your credit rating may suffer as a result of divorce. Restoring credit should begin as soon as possible. Pay your bills on the clock, cut down on debt like loans with high interest rates and credit card debt, and refrain from taking up unnecessary extra credit. A high credit score can lead to future possibilities and financial security.

- **Accumulating emergency savings:** An emergency fund provides extra financial protection when things get tight. Money uncertainty following a divorce makes setting up an emergency reserve even more significant. Try to save enough in savings to pay for a three or six-month period of spending.
- **Replenishing retirement funds:** Concentrate on replenishing your retirement resources if a divorce has depleted them. Put money into an investment account for retirement first. Compound interest allows even tiny payments to accumulate over time.
- **Reviewing insurance and your dependents:** It's important to go over and adjust the coverage and beneficiaries on your plans after a divorce. This guarantees that, in the event of your death, your assets will pass to the designated beneficiaries and that the protection you have accurately represents your actual circumstances.

Love After Losing Your Marriage

Dating after a divorce is a new territory. You might wonder, "How long should I wait before jumping into the dating scene after a divorce? When's the right time to move on?" Well, let's answer these questions and share some do's and don'ts for dating after a divorce.

Dating after an intense relationship can be emotional and complicated, but it can also be a chance for personal growth and new connections. Here are some simple tips to help you figure things out (Patton, 2020; Regan, 2020):

- **Take your time:** Don't rush into dating. Give yourself some time to heal and sort out your feelings before jumping into a new relationship. This way, you can avoid making the same mistakes again and make sure you're really ready for something new.
- **Reflect on what happened before:** Spend time thinking about your previous relationship and what you want in a new partner. This process helps you figure out what you're looking for and avoid repeating any old blunders.
- **Be truthful with yourself:** Think about whether you're really ready to start dating again and what you want from a new relationship. This honesty helps you set reasonable expectations and steer clear of heartache.
- **Take it slow:** Don't rush into things with someone new. Take your time getting to know them and don't hurry into a new relationship. This way, you can build a strong foundation and steer clear of getting hurt.
- **Get support:** Talk to friends, family, or a therapist for some advice and understanding during this time. They can help you navigate the challenges that come with dating after a tough experience.
- **Stay open-minded:** Be open to new experiences and people, even if they don't match your exact idea of what you're looking for. This approach helps you broaden your horizons and find unexpected connections.
- **Learn to connect with yourself again:** After a toxic relationship, it's important to reconnect with who you are and what you want out of life. Make sure you understand your own needs, desires, and boundaries before you re-enter the dating scene.

- **Believe in love:** It's common to feel skeptical about love after a toxic relationship, but believing that healthy and loving relationships are possible is important. Work on healing and restoring your faith in love before entering a new relationship.
- **Set healthy boundaries:** Clearly define your boundaries and communicate them openly with potential partners. This strategy can help you ensure that your needs and limits are respected in any new relationship.
- **Address intrusive thoughts:** If you find yourself struggling with intrusive thoughts or lingering trauma from the toxic relationship, consider seeking professional help to work through these challenges. Healing from past trauma is an essential step in preparing for a healthy new relationship.
- **Don't accept anything less:** Remember, you are good enough. Don't ever settle for less; don't settle for something that doesn't serve your needs. Don't settle for someone that undermines your passions and talents. Relax, you're not narcissistic; you have just learned the golden skill of valuing who and what you spend your time on.

Be good to yourself and give yourself the space you need to handle all of this. It's fine to take as much time as you need to recover and get ready for a new relationship after going through a bad experience. Prioritize your well-being and emotional health as you consider re-entering the dating world.

BREAKOUT BOX: OPENING UP TO THE FUTURE

Your past is not a place of permanent residence; rather, it is a point of reflection.

Aisha realized that she had to rediscover herself after her divorce. She found a creative way to help her approach her new journey with confidence. Just like Aisha, you need to lay an open path for yourself post-divorce.

- **Reveal your true nature:** Start by investigating pursuits and hobbies that align with your current self. Make the most of this chance to rekindle the passions that your marriage may have buried.
- **Turn off the light on the past:** Recognize that the past is not a place to live forever but a useful source of guidance and learning. Give yourself permission to let go of the past and focus on the here and now and the freedom to release old narratives and step into the present with newfound strength.
- **Handle the dating scene:** Take a proactive and self-aware approach to the idea of dating. Acknowledge the traits that are consistent with your ideals and learn how to create appropriate boundaries. The dating scene is a blank canvas on which to paint new relationships and encounters.
- **Make self-discovery a habit:** Make a conscious effort to reevaluate your identity. Think back on your goals, desires, and development as a person. Accept this time of introspection as a chance to create a life that is true to who you are.
- **Balance and limitations:** Maintain a good equilibrium between your goals for the future and your prior experiences. Set clear limits that safeguard your mental

health while keeping your mind open to future possibilities. Cheers to a future full of self-love, a revitalized sense of purpose, and the possibility of deep connections.

Recognize that the past serves as a point of reference rather than a permanent home, helping you move toward a future full of self-love, a revitalized sense of purpose, and the possibility of deep relationships. Release the burdens of the past and enter the powerful tomorrow that awaits you.

LIFE AFTER FREEDOM: REBUILDING GOALS WORKSHEET

Reclaiming your life after divorcing a narcissist.

Section 1

Reflection and self-discovery	Reflection on the past: Your answers
• Describe your emotions and thoughts about the past relationship.	
• List the lessons you've learned from the experience.	
• Strengths and achievements: Identify your strengths and achievements, both personal and professional.	
• How can you leverage these strengths to rebuild your life?	

Section 2

Emotional healing and well-being	Self-reflect and write your answers
Emotional healing • List activities or practices that bring you comfort and emotional healing. • How will you prioritize self-care in your daily life?	
Support system • Identify friends, family, or support groups that can assist you on your journey. • How will you maintain and strengthen these connections?	

Section 3

Personal development	Write down your goals
Personal growth goals • Set specific personal development goals for the next three months, six months, and year. • Consider areas such as self-confidence, resilience, and self-awareness.	
New hobbies and interests • Explore and list new hobbies or interests you'd like to pursue. • How can these activities contribute to your overall well-being?	

Section 4

Financial independence	Write down your goals and plans
Financial goals • Create short-term and long-term financial objectives. • How will you rebuild your financial stability and plan for the future?	
Budget and savings • Create a budget that aligns with your financial goals. • Pinpoint areas where you can save and invest in your future.	

Section 5

Relationship rebuilding	Write down your answers
Healthy relationship criteria • Define the qualities and values you seek in healthy relationships. • How will you ensure you maintain healthy boundaries moving forward?	
Socializing and networking • Plan activities to expand your social circle and network. • How can building new connections contribute to your personal growth?	

Section 6

Celebrating milestones	Write down your plans
Milestone celebrations • **Set small and achievable milestones for the upcoming months.** • **Plan how you'll celebrate each accomplishment along the way.**	
Positive affirmations • **Develop a list of positive affirmations to reinforce your journey.** • **How will you integrate these affirmations into your daily routine?**	

This worksheet is only an example of a guide to help you take intentional steps toward rebuilding your life after divorce. Regularly revisit your goals, celebrate your progress, and be patient with yourself throughout the process.

We're wrapping up this chapter about bouncing back after a tough divorce. Remember, the road ahead is wide open, filled with lots of new things waiting for you. You've done the groundwork for a fresh start, figured out who you really are, and learned that the past is just there to teach you, not hold you back. You have the strength to write the next exciting chapter of your life. Ready to see what's next? You deserve a life filled with joy, fulfillment, and authentic connections.

————

The sad news is that we have basically come to the end of this book. But because I don't want to leave you without all the tools you need, there is still a nice surprise left after the conclusion. But let's wrap things up first, and I'll tell you more about it.

CONCLUSION

In the complex landscape of divorce, I trust *Divorcing a Narcissist* has been a guiding light, offering a lifeline to you while you are navigating the challenging journey of breaking free from a toxic relationship. The Path to F.R.E.E.D.O.M., our comprehensive framework, has been the cornerstone of this empowering expedition, blending emotional healing with practical strategies tailored for those entangled with a narcissist.

As we reflect on the pages turned and the insights shared, the core message of this book crystallizes into a simple truth: divorcing a narcissist is more than a legal process. It's a holistic self-transformation. The Path to F.R.E.E.D.O.M., encapsulated in its seven steps, isn't just a guide; it's a blueprint for profound change.

In essence, the book's key takeaway is clear—your past does not define your future. Divorcing a narcissist is not an endpoint. Instead, it's a new beginning in your journey. There is no better time than now to face reality, rejuvenate your spirit, elevate your self-worth, empower through boundaries, determine a legal strategy, outline co-parenting plans, and finally, the most important of all—move forward.

As we bring this journey to a close, envision the possibilities that lie ahead. It's not just about overcoming the challenges posed by a narcissistic ex-spouse; it's about embracing a life that resonates with authenticity, strength, and joy. The Path to F.R.E.E.D.O.M. is a road map to a brighter, more resilient future.

It is now your moment to grab life by the handles. Use the tips and ideas you've found in this book. Be brave in facing the truth, take care of yourself, boost your confidence with self-love, set strong boundaries, make wise decisions about the legal stuff, plan co-parenting with care, and move ahead with your new strength. Persistence is important, and each tiny move matters.

Never allow anyone to define you by the shadows of your past relationships. The power to shape your life post-divorce lies within you. You have the strength to rebuild, the wisdom to heal, and the resilience to rise. Seize this moment as an opportunity for a new beginning, free from the burden of the past.

Life after divorce can take various forms. Perhaps, like Emma, you had to confront reality and rebuild your personal connections after a period of isolation. Maybe, similar to Becky, you had to pick up the pieces and find solace in self-healing by rediscovering a childhood passion, such as drawing. Or, following the example of journalist Hannah, you embarked on a new project, even traveling halfway across the world to recognize your self-worth.

Establishing boundaries became a crucial lesson for individuals like Sophia, who had to block bombarding calls from an ex and set clear communication guidelines. Alternatively, you might resonate with Carlos who had to dig into hidden financial transactions to unveil his spouse's deceitful actions.

Like Macy, you could have prioritized your children's well-being, providing them with a stable home and consistently explaining the rules. Sometimes, it's the simple things, as in Aisha's case, where decorating a new apartment served as a transformative step toward rediscovering herself.

Regardless of your unique journey, my hope is that this book has provided you with valuable insights and practical advice to navigate your future with strength and resilience.

Lastly, if this book has resonated with you, I invite you to share your thoughts and leave an honest review. Your review will not only fuel the spirit behind these words but also guide others on their journey to choose a book that offers them the support they need. Your experience could be the beacon of hope someone else longs for.

A NICE SURPRISE AWAITING YOU

Epilogue: A Love Letter

In the last part of our story, we're sharing a love letter—not to someone else, but to you. It's a celebration of your strength through the tough times and how you've become even stronger. This epilogue is all about self-love, feeling powerful, and embracing the awesome new beginnings coming your way. So, as you read this love letter, let it remind you that you're a total powerhouse, turning heartbreak into healing.

Appendix: Communication Toolkit

Before we say goodbye, check out the Communication Toolkit in the back. It's like a handy guide to help you talk effectively, whether it's with your ex, handling relationships, or just speaking up for yourself.

These practical tools are here to support you in navigating conversations with confidence. Whether you're co-parenting or just figuring things out, this toolkit is your go-to for communicating better as you keep growing and healing. Enjoy using it!

In closing, let this not be the end but a stepping stone toward the life you deserve. The path ahead is yours to walk, and the possibilities awaiting you are limitless. Embrace your newfound strength, and may your post-divorce journey be a testament to the resilience of the human spirit.

Epilogue: A Love Letter

Dear [Your Name],

As we wrap up this journey together, I've got something special for you—a love letter. Instead, you will be the one to write it to yourself. We've talked about healing and growing, and now it's time to celebrate every win and brave move you've made in life. This letter is like a big hug for your soul—a chance to recognize your strength and shower yourself with the love you truly deserve.

Why Write this Love Letter?

Life gets crazy, and we often forget to pat ourselves on the back for the good stuff. This love letter is like a friendly reminder and a powerful way to feel better. When you jot down your successes, big or small, it helps lift the weight of guilt and shame. This is your personal space to appreciate your journey, look back on moments when you were super brave, and replace any negative thoughts with a kinder view of yourself.

Let's Get Started

Think of this letter as a conversation with a friend who totally gets you, encouraging you to see your own awesomeness. Picture the letter as a warm hug, giving you comfort, recognition, and a little push to love yourself a bit more.

Examples to Spark Ideas

Remember the time you danced at a recital when you were five years old, even though you were scared? How about being there for your dog when she passed away at nine? Or when you stood up against bullying at 12? Then there was that solo trip at 19, and let's not forget launching your business at 21, even if you weren't totally sure what you were doing.

These examples are just to get you thinking. Your life is a mix of brave moments, love, and strength, and this letter is your chance to give yourself a personalized high-five.

Your Private Safe Zone

As you start pouring your thoughts onto paper, remember—this love letter is all yours. It's a cozy spot where you can be genuine without worrying about judgment. Let your words flow like you're chatting with an old friend. You're in charge of this letter, celebrating your journey and appreciating yourself.

This is your space to be kind to yourself, recognizing the challenges you've faced, the victories you've scored, and the amazing person you've become. Your love letter is like a mirror showing off the incredible spirit in you, a reminder that you're worthy of loads of self-love.

As you wrap up this writing adventure, see it as a fresh start. Look at yourself with love and pride. Embrace the awesome person you are, because you truly deserve it.

End your letter with an appropriate and warm ending, such as this example:

With Love and Celebration,

[Your Name]

If you like, write it with your favorite pen on a decorative piece of paper, and keep it safe where you can always look at it as a reminder of the gift of your precious life.

Appendix: Communication Toolkit

Empowering responses for navigating communication with a narcissistic spouse or ex-spouse.

Introduction

Communicating with a narcissistic spouse or ex-spouse can be an uphill battle, often leading to conflict and emotional strain. This appendix serves as a practical guide, offering ready-to-use responses designed to minimize conflict, establish clear boundaries, and safeguard your emotional well-being. These responses act as tools to help you navigate conversations with a narcissistic person effectively, reducing stress and maintaining control over your interactions.

Purpose of Prepared Responses

The purpose of these prepared responses is to equip you with effective communication strategies. With these tools at your disposal, you can navigate conversations confidently, minimize unnecessary conflict, and protect your emotional well-being.

KEY CONSIDERATIONS

Before delving into the toolkit, keep the following points in mind:

- **Flexibility:** These responses are starting points and can be adapted based on your specific circumstances. You are welcome to change them according to your specific challenge or situation.
- **Empowerment:** You have the power to set boundaries and control the tone of your interactions. These responses are tools to empower you in managing communication with a narcissistic ex-spouse.

TOOLKIT RESPONSES

Responding to Impossible Co-Parenting Dilemmas

When faced with challenging co-parenting situations, maintaining composure is crucial. Use the following responses to navigate impossible co-parenting dilemmas:

Dealing with accusations

- "I appreciate your concern. Let's focus on [specific co-parenting matter] to ensure [child's name] has the best experience with both of us."
- "I get where you're coming from. Let's figure out a solution that's good for [child's name] and makes co-parenting work well for both of us."
- "I hear what you're saying. Let's team up to sort this out and make sure [child's name] has the best time with both of us."

Setting boundaries

- "I understand your perspective. To keep things clear, let's communicate through [preferred method] and stick to discussing [child-related topics]."
- "I hear your concerns. Let's agree to communicate through [preferred method] and limit our discussions to matters directly related to [child's name]'s well-being and upbringing."
- "I understand where you're coming from. Moving forward, let's use [preferred method] for our communications and focus solely on topics that directly impact [child's name]."

Mastering the Art of Canned Responses

Canned responses provide a strategic way to handle common scenarios. Utilize these scripts to maintain control over your communication:

Gray rock technique

- "I see your point. Let's keep our discussions focused on [specific topic]."
- "I understand your perspective. Let's keep our discussions focused on [specific topic] to maintain a constructive co-parenting dynamic."
- "I hear what you're saying. Let's prioritize [specific topic] in our conversations to support a positive co-parenting environment."

Disengaging from manipulation

- "I value open communication. If you have concerns about [topic], let's address them calmly and respectfully."
- "I think we need to have an open conversation. If there's something bothering you about [topic], let's discuss it calmly and respectfully so we can keep our co-parenting relationship healthy."
- "I appreciate your input. Let's ensure that our discussions about [topic] are conducted in a respectful and constructive manner to benefit our co-parenting efforts."

Navigating Communication with Narcissists

For a comprehensive approach, explore these responses to effectively navigate communication:

- **Redirecting conversations:** Handling discussions with a narcissist often requires a delicate touch. Instead of succumbing to potential negativity, employ the redirection technique:
- "I understand your perspective. Can we shift the conversation to [neutral topic] to keep things constructive?"

By subtly steering the dialogue toward a neutral ground, you maintain control over the tone and content of the discussion. This strategy not only helps in avoiding unnecessary conflict but also opens the door to more constructive communication.

- **Affirming your boundaries:** Affirming your boundaries is crucial when dealing with a narcissistic ex-spouse. This response is a gentle yet firm way to assert your need for personal space:

- "I need some space to process this. Let's revisit the discussion when we can communicate more calmly."
- **Laying a foundation for better future communication:** Setting boundaries is an act of self-preservation. By expressing the need for a calm space, you protect your emotional well-being and lay the foundation for more productive conversations in the future.

Managing Your Emotions When You're Dealing With the Narcissist

Let's face it: dealing with a narcissist can drive you crazy and make you (and your child) very mad. So, it actually affects your nervous system, and you fail to remain grounded. The moment you don't feel safe anymore, you are triggered to your "flight" or "fight" response, and you get edgy and anxious. That's your nervous system trying to take care of you. But if it continues, you may go into the freeze position where you are tired and have lost your energy so much that you can't pursue the situation any further.

You need to self-regulate yourself and teach your children to regulate themselves, too. This will help you respond better and build resilience in your nervous system to deal with these challenges.

Responses In-the-Moment to Regulate Your Emotions

- Here are some communication responses for managing your emotions when dealing with a narcissist:
- "I know we might not agree on everything, but let's work together to find a solution that works for both of us and keeps things positive."
- "Thanks for sharing your thoughts, but let's stick to talking about [specific topic] in a respectful and helpful way."

- "I hear your concerns, so let's figure out how we can talk in a way that works for both of us and keeps things positive for everyone."
- "I like being open, but let's make sure our talks stay focused on [specific topic] and stay respectful and helpful."
- Together with this strategy, employ self-help techniques to keep yourself calm. When you feel dysregulated, you need to employ techniques as your soldiers to protect you. Remember to try deep breathing, remove yourself from the situation for a short while, or think about something else for a second to calm you and help you focus.

Navigating communication with a narcissistic spouse or ex-spouse is undeniably challenging, but employing strategic responses can make a significant difference.

This Communication Toolkit is a resource to empower you in managing communication with a narcissistic ex-spouse. Remember, adaptability is key, and these responses are tools to help you navigate conversations effectively. You need to alter it to help you in your unique situation.

By setting clear boundaries and maintaining control over your interactions, you can protect your emotional well-being and foster a healthier communication dynamic. May these responses serve as a guide on your journey to reclaiming control and building resilience in the face of challenging interactions.

In conclusion, recognize that effective communication with a narcissist involves a delicate balance of asserting boundaries and redirecting conversations toward constructive topics. By integrating these responses into your toolkit, you not only navigate the challenges more effectively but also pave the way for healthier interactions, ultimately contributing to your overall well-being. Remember, these responses are tools—adapt them to your unique situation, and let them be your allies in the journey toward positive communication.

References

Abuse Warrior. (2021, March 20). *41 manipulation tactics used by narcissists, psychopaths, and sociopaths*. https://abusewarrior.com/abuse/manipulation-tactics

Akin, E. (2022) 10 Ways to Build Self-Esteem After Narcissistic Abuse. Unfilteredd. https://unfilteredd.net/10-ways-to-build-self-esteem-after-2experiencing-narcissistic-abuse

Anwar, B. (2022, February 4). *Ask a therapist: "How to set boundaries with a narcissist."* Talkspace. https://www.talkspace.com/mental-health/conditions/articles/how-to-set-boundaries-with-a-narcissist/

Arabi, S. (2019, May 29). *5 common struggles children of narcissists face in adulthood.* Psych Central. https://psychcentral.com/blog/recovering-narcissist/2019/05/5-common-struggles-children-of-narcissists-face-in-adulthood#1

Arzt, N. (2023, August 23). *15 tips for recovering from narcissistic abuse.* Choosing Therapy. https://www.choosingtherapy.com/recovering-from-narcissistic-abuse/

AZ Family Law Lawyers (n.d.). *Manipulation tactics that narcissists use in divorce.* https://azfamilylawlawyer.com/manipulation-tactics-that-narcissists-use-in-divorce

Biggers, L. (2022, December 15). *9 signs of narcissistic personality disorder.* Duke Health. https://www.dukehealth.org/blog/9-signs-of-narcissistic-personality-disorder

Bockmann, M. (2020, October 22). *5 tips for dating again after leaving A toxic relationship.* YourTango. https://www.yourtango.com/experts/mitzi-bockmann/how-take-first-step-dating-after-leaving-toxic-relationship

Brown, AJP. (n.d). *Rediscovering YOU - Life after divorce.* Amanda JP Brown. https://www.amandajpbrown.com/blog/rediscovering-you

Brown, M. (2023, January 14). Signs you're co-parenting with a narcissist—and what to do. Parents.com. https://www.parents.com/parenting/how-to-know-if-you-re-co-parenting-with-a-narcissist-and-what-to-do-about-it/

Buchanan, R. B.(2023, June 26). *Narcissist divorce strategies: tips for a successful outcome.* https://www.rbbfirm.com/narcissist-divorce-strategies/

Caligor, E., & Petrini, M. J. (2022, October 21). *Narcissistic personality disorder: Epidemiology, pathogenesis, clinical manifestations, course, assessment, and diagnosis.* UpToDate. https://www.uptodate.com/contents/narcissistic-personality-disorder-epidemiology-pathogenesis-clinical-manifestations-course-assessment-and-diagnosis

Cascioli, R. (2022, February 24). *Those who hope for peace by preparing for war are deluded.* New Daily Compass. https://newdailycompass.com/en/those-who-hope-for-peace-by-preparing-for-war-are-deluded

Charlie, G. (2016, November 15). *I dated a narcissist & it destroyed my self-confidence.* Bolde. https://www.bolde.com/dated-narcissist-destroyed-self-confidence/

Cikanavicius, D. (2019, October 20). *Triangulation: The narcissists best play.* Psych Central. https://psychcentral.com/blog/psychology-self/2019/10/triangulation-and-narcissism

Communication in a parallel parenting arrangement (n.d.). *Our Family Wizard Blog.* https://www.ourfamilywizard.com/blog/communication-parallel-parenting-arrangement

Corelli, C. (2023a, September 20). Toxic things a narcissist will say to destroy your confidence. https://www.carlacorelli.com/narcissistic-abuse-recovery/toxic-things-a-narcissist-will-say-to-destroy-your-confidence

Corelli, C. (2023b, December 23). *Narcissistic family roles – the complicated dynamics of narcissistic families.* https://www.carlacorelli.com/narcissistic-abuse-recovery/narcissistic-family-roles-the-complicated-dynamics-of-narcissistic-families/

Corelli, C. (2023c, December 25). *How to set boundaries with narcissists—strengthen Your defences.* Carla Corelli. https://www.carlacorelli.com/narcissism-glossary/boundaries-narcissist/

Craft, K. (2022, April 15). *How to spot manipulation tactics.* Psych Central. https://psychcentral.com/lib/tactics-manipulators-use-to-win-and-confuse-you

Cuncic, A. (2023, November 06). *Effects of narcissistic abuse.* VeryWell Mind. https://www.verywellmind.com/effects-of-narcissistic-abuse-5208164

@dealwithnarcissist. (2019, December 18). Self-worth, appreciation, ego and narcissism. *Deal with Narcissist Blog.* https://www.dealwithnarcissist.com/self-worth-appreciation-ego-and-narcissism

Durvasula, R. (2021, June 15). *8 strategies to help your child cope with a narcissistic parent.* Talking Parents. https://talkingparents.com/parenting-resources/help-your-child-cope-with-narcissistic-parent

Empathic Warrior. (2023, July 13). *5 reasons why narcissists hate boundaries.* https://medium.com/@empathicwarrior/5-reasons-why-narcissist-hate-boundaries

Farzad, B. (n.d.). *How to protect your child from a narcissistic parent | narcissistic abuse guide for parents.* Farzad & Ochoa Family Law Attorneys. https://farzadlaw.com/divorcing-a-narcissist/how-protect-child-narcissistic-father-mother#

Firestone, L. (2013, April 29). *In a relationship with a narcissist? A guide to narcissistic relationships.* PsychAlive. https://www.psychalive.org/narcissistic-relationships/

Fletcher, J. (2022, March 28). Divorce grief: Mourning your marriage. Psych Central. https://psychcentral.com/blog/how-to-grieve-after-divorce

Gillis, K. (2022, November 10). *9 narcissistic manipulation tactics & how to deal.* Choosing Therapy. https://www.choosingtherapy.com/narcissistic-manipulation-tactics/

Gillis, K. (2023, June 14). *16 signs of narcissistic abuse & victim syndrome.* Choosing Therapy. https://www.choosingtherapy.com/narcissistic-abuse-syndrome/

Goal setting for life post-divorce worksheet (n.d). Hello Divorce. https://20830915.fs1.

hubspotusercontent-na1.net/hubfs/20830915/Downloads/Generic/Divorce% 20Goal-Setting%20Worksheet.pdf

Gold Buscho, A. (2021, September 28). *When will the grief after divorce end?* Psychology Today. https://www.psychologytoday.com/us/blog/better-divorce/ 202109/when-will-the-grief-after-divorce-end

Grande, D. (2022, September 9). *11 signs of a narcissistic relationship & how to cope.* Choosing Therapy. https://www.choosingtherapy.com/narcissistic-relationship/

Grande, D. (2023, June 7). 15 tips for setting boundaries with a narcissist. Choosing Therapy. https://www.choosingtherapy.com/setting-boundaries-with-a-narcissist/

Grice, J. (n.d.). "Parallel parenting" when co-parenting doesn't work with a narcissist | surviving + thriving after divorce. Surviving + Thriving after Divorce. https:// jengrice.com/parallel-parenting-when-co-parenting-doesnt-work-with-a-narcissist/

The Harris Law Firm (2023, May 27). Charting the course to financial recovery after divorce https://www.harrislawtx.com/blog/2023/05/charting-the-course-to-finan cial-recovery-after-divorce/

Heather R Hayes & Associates. (2023, September 22). *The impact of growing up with a narcissistic parent.* https://www.heatherhayes.com/the-impact-of-growing-up-with-a-narcissistic-parent

Hill, L. (n.d). *Co-parenting with a Narcissist?* Divorce Strategies Northwest. https:// www.divorcestrategiesnw.com/2020/05/co-parenting-with-a-narcissist/

Holland, M. (2022, August 18). 15 signs you're married to a narcissist & what to do about it. Choosing Therapy. https://www.choosingtherapy.com/married-to-a-narcissist/

Holland, K. (2023, May 17). *Stages of grief: General patterns for breakups, divorce, loss, more.* Healthline. https://www.healthline.com/health/stages-of-grief#7-stages

Hutchinson, T. (2016). https://www.drtracyhutchinson.com/what-are-personal-boundaries-and-why-are-they-important

Jack, C. (2020, April 16). How to Develop a Sense of Self After Narcissistic Abuse. Psychology Today. https://www.psychologytoday.com/intl/blog/women-autism-spectrum-disorder/202004/how-develop-sense-self-after-narcissistic-abuse

Jensen, K. (2023, May 12). *Setting healthy boundaries: A key to improving mental health.* Recovery Ways Blog. https://www.recoveryways.com/rehab-blog/setting-healthy-boundaries-a-key-to-improving-mental-health/

Joubert, J. (n.d.). *Quote: "Children need models rather than critics".* Brainy Quote. https://www.brainyquote.com/quotes/joseph_joubert_103419

Judge Anthony (n.d.). Beat a narcissist in court. https://www.judgeanthony.com/

Kassel, G. (2022, December 7). *9 signs you're dating a narcissist — and how to deal with them.* Healthline. https://www.healthline.com/health/mental-health/am-i-dating-a-narcissist#charming-first-impression

Kolyanne. (2023, December 25). *Narcissist parent: Insight into my healing journey & lessons.* Pinch of Attitude. https://www.pinchofattitude.com/narcissist-parent/

Laderer, A. (n.d.). Therapy that will actually help you heal from narcissistic abuse.

Charlie Health. https://www.charliehealth.com/post/what-is-the-best-therapy-for-narcissistic-abuse

Leonard, K., Watts, R. (2022, May 4). *The ultimate guide to S.M.A.R.T goals*. Forbes. https://www.forbes.com/advisor/business/smart-goals/

The Little Shaman. (2018, February 1). Narcissists hate boundaries. *HubPages*. https://discover.hubpages.com/health/Narcissists-Hate-Boundaries

Lloyd, Platt & Co. (n.d.). How to divorce a narcissist. https://www.divorcesolicitors.com/how-to-divorce-a-narcissist/

MindWell Psychology NYC. (2022, July 30). *How to protect a child from a narcissistic father*. https://mindwellnyc.com/how-to-protect-child-from-narcissistic-father/

Mafi, T. (n.d.). *Quote: "Moving forward is the only way to survive."* Quotefancy. https://quotefancy.com/quote/43000/Tahereh-Mafi-Moving-forward-is-the-only-way-to-survive

McGee, J. (2023, April 12). How to reclaim your identity after narcissistic abuse. Jim McGee Coaching. https://jimmcgeecoaching.com/identity-after-narcissistic-abuse

Medina Family Law Associates (2023, October 1). Dealing with challenges when divorcing a narcissist. https://www.richardnelsonllp.co.uk/divorcing-a-narcissist-7-strategies-to-help-in-the-legal-proceedings/

Neuharth, D. (2017, September 8). 12 classic propaganda techniques narcissists use to manipulate you. Choosing Therapy. https://www.choosingtherapy.com/narcissistic-manipulation-tactics

Newport Institute. (2022, November 1). How having a narcissistic parent impacts young adult mental health. https://www.newportinstitute.com/resources/mental-health/narcissistic-parent/

Porrey, M. (2021, November 29). Working through grief after divorce. Verywell Health. https://www.verywellhealth.com/divorce-grief-5208157

Raypole, C. (2021, May 19) Narcissistic traits: Beyond a sense of superiority. Psych Central. https://psychcentral.com/disorders/narcissistic-personality-disorder/narcissistic-traits

Robinson, K. M. (n.d.). *What to do if you're co-parenting with a narcissist*. WebMD. https://www.webmd.com/mental-health/features/narcissistic-coparent

Roy, S. (2023, December 13). Divorce a covert narcissist: Tips to survive, traps to avoid. *The Happiness Blog*. https://happyproject.in/surviving-covert-narcissist-divorce-tactics/

SAS for Women. (2019, October 23). *What does finding ourselves after divorce mean & is it actually possible?* Support and Solutions for Thriving after Divorce (SAS). https://sasforwomen.com/what-does-finding-ourselves-after-divorce-mean-is-it-actually-possible

Sember, B. (2023). Finding yourself after divorce: 10 actionable tips. Divorce.com. https://divorce.com/blog/finding-yourself-after-divorce/

Stoneson, A. (2014, May 20). *Boundaries matter. Here's why.* Labyrinth Healing. http://labyrinthhealing.com/blog/boundaries-matter-heres-why

Telloian, C. (2021, September 15). *How many types of narcissism are there?* Psych Central. https://psychcentral.com/health/types-of-narcissism#5-types-of-narcissism

Therapy for narcissistic abuse: The 5 best affordable alternatives (n.d.). Trigger Your Trip. https://triggeryourtrip.com/emotional-path/therapy-for-narcissistic-abuse/

Taylor, H. (n.d.). *Charting your divorce course.* https://heleneltaylor.com/charting-your-divorce-course/

Thomas, N. (2023, June 27). Narcissistic parents: Traits, signs, & how to deal with one. Choosing Therapy. https://www.choosingtherapy.com/narcissistic-parent/

Trepany, C. (2023, August 15). *What happens when a narcissist becomes a parent?* USA Today. https://www.usatoday.com/story/life/health-wellness/2023/08/15/narcissism-and-parenting-narcissistic-parents-cast-kids-into-roles/70591780007/

Villines, Z. (2023, September 20). *Examples of narcissistic behavior in relationships.* Medical News Today. https://www.medicalnewstoday.com/articles/example-of-narcissistic-behavior

Wakefield, M. (2023, July 15). *The cycle of narcissistic abuse.* Narcissistic Abuse Rehab. https://www.narcissisticabuserehab.com/cycle-of-narcissistic-abuse/

Wolf, J. (2020, July 24). *Factors used to determine the custody of children.* Verywell Family. https://www.verywellfamily.com/factors-that-determine-child-custody-2997640

Washington, D. (2022, October 25). *How to win full custody of your child.* Verywell Family. https://www.verywellfamily.com/how-to-win-full-custody-of-your-child-2997293

What are the challenges of divorcing a narcissist? (2022, June 27). Rech Law. https://www.rechlaw.com/blog/2022/june/what-are-the-challenges-of-divorcing-a-narcissis/

What to expect when divorcing a narcissist. (2021, January 30). Sullivan Law. https://sullivan-law.com/what-to-expect-when-divorcing-a-narcissist/

Wroldson, G. (n.d.). *How-To protect your kids from gaslighting.* https://gracewroldson.com/how-to-protect-your-kids-from-gaslighting-and-the-lies-of-the-narcissistic-parent/

www.ingramcontent.com/pod-product-compliance
Lightning Source LLC
Chambersburg PA
CBHW070714130626
46553CB00005B/1989